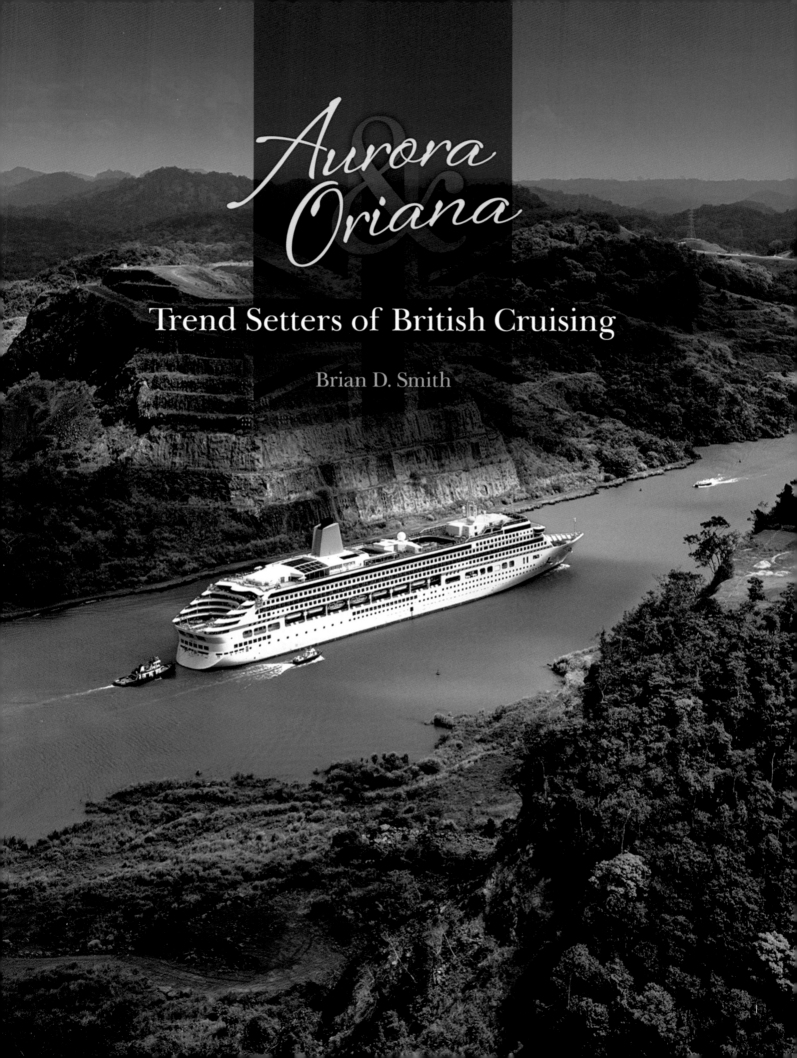

Aurora & Oriana

Trend Setters of British Cruising

Brian D. Smith

*Title page: The **Aurora** is seen on her annual world cruise passing through the Panama Canal on her journey from the Atlantic to the Pacific Ocean. (P&O Cruises)*

*Below: The **Aurora** is guided into place in one of the three sets of locks needed on the Panama Canal to raise the ship through the undulated terrain which the canal traverses as well as the 20cm difference in sea level between the Atlantic and Pacific Oceans. (P&O Cruises)*

Ferry
Publications

Published by:
Ferry Publications, PO Box 33, Ramsey, Isle of Man IM99 4LP
Tel: +44 (0) 1624 898445   Fax: +44 (0) 1624 898449
E-mail: ferrypubs@manx.net   Website: www.ferrypubs.co.uk

Contents

Produced and designed by Ferry Publications trading as Lily Publications Ltd

PO Box 33, Ramsey, Isle of Man, British Isles, IM99 4LP

Tel: +44 (0) 1624 898446   Fax: +44 (0) 1624 898449

www.ferrypubs.co.uk e-mail: info@lilypublications.co.uk

Printed and bound by Gomer Press Ltd., Wales, UK +44 (0) 1559 362371 © Lily Publications 2012

First Published: May 2012

*Sailing into a beautiful sunset, the **Oriana** is on top of the world as she leaves one of the Norwegian Fjords whilst on a cruise close to the Arctic Circle. (P&O Cruises)*

Foreword

BY CAROL MARLOW, MANAGING DIRECTOR P&O CRUISES

ORIANA and *Aurora* were the first of the new generation of ships built for the P&O Cruises fleet, when the recent growth of British cruising really started in 1995-2000. Named by royalty, both are great ships that have earned their place as part of P&O Cruises' heritage. The best known of our ships since Canberra, they embody all that is P&O Cruises - the trust, Britishness and aspirational standards our customers have come to expect.

This book talks about the building and adventures of both these ships, and for those involved, is a step back in time.

When I joined the company, *Oriana* was already our flagship, and *Aurora* was being designed for the new millenium. She was to be brighter and bolder than her sister, and whilst she was to be a ship tailored for the British market, she would also command international renown.

Today, both these ships are still firm favourites of our loyal passengers, seen as ships built to last, full of character and memories

I hope you enjoy this insight into two of our most famous ships.

Carol Marlow
Managing Director, P&O Cruises

Introduction

The Peninsular and Oriental Steam Navigation Company was one of Britain's leading passenger shipping companies of the 19th and 20th centuries. From humble beginnings in 1837, when the company was first formed to take the British Royal Mail to the Iberian Peninsula, it soon grew into a major player in the passenger shipping industry with large modern steam-powered ships sailing to the Orient, India and other destinations in the British Empire.

Its two founders, Brodie McGhie Willcox and Arthur Anderson, were visionaries who saw that the future of world shipping was with steam-powered ships and guaranteed timetables whilst many of their competitors resisted this untested science and continued to offer passage by sail with no guaranteed arrival date. Not only

was the company credited with revolutionising the way ordinary people looked at travelling by sea but also with persuading the Royal Navy that the future of Britain's sea defences and its place as a world power would depend on the Admiralty replacing its aging fleet of sailing ships with newer steam-powered vessels. In two World Wars and in other conflicts, most recently the Falkland Islands of 1982, P&O has answered the call of its country and supported the military in the most exemplary fashion. Who will ever forget the television pictures of the cruise ship *Canberra* and the car ferry *Norland* in San Carlos Water, right in the heart of the battle and with P&O crews on board!

Today the cruise ship division of the old P&O company is owned by the American cruise giant Carnival

*A huge flotilla of yachts and other pleasure craft join the **Oriana** as she arrives in Sydney Harbour for the first time in 1996. (P&O Cruises)*

Corporation and is marketed as P&O Cruises. The company is without doubt Britain's leading cruise line with seven beautiful ships offering more destinations than any other UK cruise operator. The contemporary story of the company starts in 1995 with the introduction of their first ever purpose-built cruise ship, the *Oriana*, and her near sister, the *Aurora*, five years later. Built by the German shipyard of Meyer Werft, it was these two incredible ships on which the foundations of today's successful company were built. With their beautifully raked sterns, expansive outside deck spaces and gleaming white hulls they are the epitome of how a traditional British cruise ship should look.

Such is the pace of change in the cruise industry that in the five years between the two ships entering service, the demands from the cruise passenger and the advances in marine engineering meant that the newer *Aurora* would be rather more different than anyone could have imagined. This book explains how each ship was designed and constructed and why both have built up such a large and dedicated number of passengers who love sailing on them.

Brian D. Smith
London
April 2012.

Setting the Scene

Today, P&O Cruises is a very successful British company owning seven ships, all dedicated to the British cruise market and sailing to various locations all around the world. They have a proud and interesting history which can be traced back to the early 19th century when in 1815 Brodie McGhie Willcox started trading as a shipbroker in a small office, close to the River Thames in the centre of London. Not a great deal is known about how well Willcox did in these early years but he clearly traded with some success as in 1822 he had the need to employ a young clerk from the Shetland Islands by the name of Arthur Anderson who had served with the Royal Navy during the Napoleonic Wars and therefore had some important maritime experience to add to the company. Such was Anderson's drive and enthusiasm that within three years of joining the company, Willcox decided to make him a partner and in 1825 the two of them started trading as Willcox and Anderson. Not only did they act as shipbrokers, they actually became shipowners after a small American schooner had gone aground near Dover and her owners had wanted to sell the wreck to limit the liability of the damaged ship. Once Willcox and Anderson had purchased the vessel, they repaired her and fitted her with some defensive armaments before sending her on her first journey for the company to Portugal carrying various cargoes and a small number of passengers. The name of this ship is not known but it began a dynasty that continues today in the form of P&O Cruises.

During this period Portugal was involved in a civil war and Anderson began the very dangerous and risky business of gun running for the Portuguese Crown and its supporters, which included an elderly British Admiral by the name of Sir Charles Napier who later worked for Anderson. The decision proved to be a wise one as the Queen of Portugal won her war and rewarded Willcox and Anderson with contracts to serve her country from the UK. No sooner had the war in Portugal finished than a further civil war broke out in Spain. Again Willcox and Anderson sided with the legitimate Queen and once again backed the winning side. This was to be of great importance to the company in later years as the Spanish Ambassador in London would use great influence to help the company win new contracts to the Iberian Peninsula.

SAIL GIVES WAY TO STEAM

At this time there were a number of great and famous men who were starting shipping companies using steamships, including Isambard Kingdom Brunel who was running a single ship service across the Atlantic to New York with his latest ground breaking vessel, the *Great Western*. The problem was that steamships were still in their infancy and were extremely unreliable. When ships broke down there was more often than not, nothing to replace them with and Anderson quickly realised that for a

shipping company to succeed it needed to have a fleet of vessels which included a spare ship ready to enter service if required. In 1834 they decided to rebrand their company with an eye to making it the premier company taking cargo and passengers to the Iberian Peninsula. A prospectus was issued with the company name of The Peninsular Steam Navigation Company, the Oriental suffix was added later when they began to explore routes into the Mediterranean and across to Egypt.

In 1835, the Spanish Ambassador in London took steps to introduce the benefits of a reliable steamship service to Spain and chartered several steamships from the Dublin & London Steam Packet Company. He did not forget the involvement of Willcox and Anderson in supporting the Spanish Queen a few years before and so placed the management of this new venture under the Peninsular Steam Navigation Company.

To supplement this additional trade, the company purchased a 206-ton paddle steamer called the *William Fawcett* which had been built in Liverpool in 1828. With two large sails and twin paddle wheels, she had been named after the engineer who had built her engines and is regarded as being the first ship to be actually owned by the Peninsular Steam Navigation Company. To give some idea of comparisons, the *William Fawcett* was less than 100 metres long and her engines had a total output of around 60 horsepower. P&O Cruises' latest ship, the *Azura*, is almost 300 metres long, 120,000 gross tons and her engines have a total power output closer to 100,000 horsepower.

By 1837 Willcox and Anderson owned a fleet of seven steamships which were all fitted with auxiliary sails whilst most ships at this time were sail ships with auxiliary steam engines. They had many competitors who were struggling to make their steamships pay but Anderson believed that if they could offer a regular service which would leave exactly when advertised and arrive at its destination at a designated time then people would be willing to pay the extra needed to make this service viable. It is important to remember that at this time, most services were dependent on the wind and tide and timetables were little more than a planner's dream. With the strong currents in the English Channel and the heavy seas of the Bay of Biscay it could take anything up to ten days for a ship to reach Portugal from London and on occasions even three weeks could be the norm.

A TIMETABLED SERVICE

Clearly matters had to improve and Anderson realised that if he could reduce these times and provide a reliable service then his new company was in with a chance of success. It was decided to advertise a sailing from Falmouth to Vigo in Spain that would take only 54 hours, an unbelievably quick time for the period. There would be a

An oil painting by T.F. Dicksee showing P&O's co-founder and Chairman Arthur Anderson in 1850. (Ferry Publications Library)

Brodie McGhie Willcox, also painted by T.F. Dicksee in 1850. (Ferry Publications Library)

*Captain Richard Bourne, owner of the **William Fawcett**, who collaborated with Anderson and Willcox in creating P&O. (Ferry Publications Library)*

sailing connection to London which would take another two days but they were offering a real timetable from England to Spain which was significantly less than anyone else could ever hope to offer. Willcox was still worried about making such a business profitable but Anderson convinced him that if they could win another large contract delivering goods to the continent then the business would be a success. The suggestion came from Richard Bourne, one of the company's senior employees who had joined them in 1835 from the Dublin & London Steam Packet Company. Bourne convinced Willcox and Anderson that the way to make their new company profitable was to win the Royal Mail contract to Spain and Portugal. He believed that any company that took the Royal Mail across the sea always made a profit. The current contract to run the mail was up for renewal so Willcox immediately put plans together ready to tender the Admiralty when the contract was advertised. After many deliberations between the three executive figures of the Peninsular Steam Navigation Company, they managed to offer the Admiralty a fixed timetabled service for which they would charge the Government £30,000 per annum to take the Royal Mail to the Iberian Peninsula.

The Admiralty were reluctant to do business with the three men but Willcox, by now an MP, managed to convince the Government that they could do the job safely and reliably. No one else could match the price or delivery times that Willcox and Anderson were offering so on 22nd August 1837, the new contract to carry the Royal Mail to Iberia was duly signed. This is now regarded as the official beginning of the company which today trades as

P&O Cruises. On 1st September, the largest ship in the fleet, the 450-ton *Don Juan* left England bound for Spain carrying the first cargo belonging to the Royal Mail and on board were Anderson and his wife Mary Ann. The operation with the Royal Mail was so successful that within a year the Government asked the company to make plans for taking the mail from Gibraltar right through to Alexandria in Egypt. The importance of winning this contract could not be underestimated as the significance of Alexandria was not the mail or the trade to Egypt itself but the fact it was the next staging post for the lucrative mail run to India and the countries beyond the subcontinent.

TO THE ORIENT

The Suez Canal, linking the Mediterranean to the Red Sea, was still some time from being completed by the French and it was not until 1869 that it was open for traffic. In the 1830s it involved ships docking at Alexandria or Cairo before their passengers and cargo continued their journey across the Isthmus of Suez, a slow and sometimes dangerous desert journey of 150 miles on camel or donkey. One of the reasons that the British Government gave the Alexandria contract to the Peninsular Steam Navigation Company was that they promised to send the mail in modern steamers calling at British ports such as Gibraltar and Malta on the way. Others sent the mail partly across land and France in particular. There was never any evidence that the French authorities interfered with the British Mail but Britain had been at war with France for as long as anyone could remember and there were many

members of the British Government who were not yet ready to trust the French with the British Royal Mail.

To take on this extra work the company needed additional ships and employees but before it could do this it required incorporation by Royal Charter which would basically grant the company Limited status. It finally received this in December 1840 alongside a new set of directors with Willcox and Anderson remaining as Managing Directors. The name Oriental was officially added to the company's name and from this point on it was known as the Peninsular and Oriental Steam Navigation Company or, more affectionately as P&O for short. In exchange for shares, the company acquired a ship from a trans-Atlantic company who had run into difficulties after one of its competitors, Samuel Cunard, had won the Atlantic Royal Mail contract. It is interesting to see that Richard Bourne was completely right in his prediction that any company that won the contract to carry the Royal Mail had a greater chance of success as today, albeit in a significantly different form, the only two significant shipping companies that were trading in the 1830s and still survive in the 21st century are P&O Cruises and Cunard; both of whom had Royal Mail contracts from the British Government.

In the 1840s, the only company taking the Royal Mail to India was the powerful East India Company whose Royal Charter went right back to the times of Queen Elizabeth I. They controlled all the mail from Bombay to the UK and were not about to give up this very lucrative trade without a fight.

The terms of P&O's Charter were that it could take the mail to India but it did not state what part of India. Rather than cause friction with a registered heavy weight company with influential friends, P&O decided to send the Royal Mail to Calcutta. The problem with this was that most passengers wanted to go to Bombay and not Calcutta and had been used to extremely lavish ships offering a great deal of comfort; albeit that they were still powered by sail and very slow. To compete, P&O were going to have to build at least two new and very large, comfortable steamships that were capable of taking a combination of passengers and cargo to run between Suez and India. By running a steamship service so far from home, P&O were coming up against a set of logistics that had never been encountered before.

In those days it was not just a question of fuelling and storing in England, then setting sail and arriving in India a few weeks later as there were no established places to take on additional coal and provisions. Sailing ships carrying coal had to be dispatched in advance to various locations on the route to await the steamer where it would then refuel. The sailing ships would also carry agents to these locations where they would arrange to purchase fresh water, food and other provisions.

The new ships would cost £60,000 each and would be wooden paddle steamers of around 2,000 tons with a length of 240 feet. Each would have 60 cabins and berths for 150 people. They were elegant ships with three masts of sail and two funnels. They had clipper bows and wide stern windows. The normal arrangement for passenger ships of the time was to have the public rooms in the centre of the ship with the cabins at the forward and after ends. P&O decided to reverse this with large passenger rooms at the bow and stern and the cabins running in the middle of the ship, the idea being that in rough weather the centre of the ship tends to move around less and therefore when people were resting in their cabins they would have a more comfortable passage.

The first of the new ships, the *Hindonstan*, sailed from Southampton for India on 24th September 1842 via Gibraltar, St Vincent, Ascension Island, Cape Town, Mauritius and Ceylon taking a total of 91 days. Upon her arrival she immediately set sail for Suez on what was to be her regular route via Madras, Ceylon and Aden. The second ship was named the *Bentinck* and joined her sister in the following year. P&O could now take the Royal Mail and passengers from London to India using the *Great Liverpool* or the *Oriental* from England to Alexandria before everyone went across land to Suez where they would pick up one of the new ships on to India. The journey times were significantly shorter than those being offered by the East India Company who could still take up to a year to reach India, going around the Cape of Good Hope in South Africa.

GROWING THE PASSENGER TRADE

After winning the new mail contracts to India, Willcox and Anderson looked at new ways to increase the profitability of their company without the need for any additional expenditure. Anderson managed to convince Willcox that people would be willing to pay good money to travel on their steamships and to visit the many interesting ports and countries that P&O traded with. It was another imaginative idea which he had originally conceived back in 1835 when he ran a small newspaper in the Shetland Isles called the 'Shetland Journal'. In one particular issue there was empty advertising space which Anderson had been very keen to fill up by any means necessary. So he used it to advertised 'Ghost' cruises on local ships plying the waters around the Shetland Islands that didn't even exist.

However, it was not until 1844 that the first ever real cruise was advertised in the British press, sailing from England to the Mediterranean and such exotic destinations as Malta, Athens and Rhodes.

The novelist William Makepeace Thackery was given a complimentary ticket by P&O on one of their first ever cruises as a way of obtaining free advertising for the new

*Top: In 1835 the **William Fawcett** was charted to open services to Spain and Portugal. (Ferry Publications Library)*

*Above left: A lithograph by J.I. Herdman depicting the Mediterranean service liner **Great Liverpool**, ex **Liverpool**, as she appeared in 1840. (Ferry Publications Library)*

*Above right: P&O's **Vectis** was converted for cruise operations in 1904 and renamed the **Rome**. (Ferry Publications Library).*

venture. He wrote the book 'Notes of a Journey from Cornhill to Grand Cairo' under the pseudonym of Michael Angelo Titmarsh and travelled on several ships, including the *Lady Mary Wood*, the *Tagus* and the *Iberia* to Gibraltar, Greece and Egypt, all of which were scheduled services rather than a leisurely cruise to those destinations. Thackery was very grateful to P&O for their kindness and wrote very highly of them, if not the places that he visited, but the stategy worked and P&O had their free publicity. P&O's network of Mediterranean and Black Sea routes continued to build in the 1840s, including a route to Constantinople. However, these were not as successful as the routes to India and the east so some of them were dropped in favour of the more lucrative Royal Mail services.

The start of the Crimean War in 1853 put a stop to any cruise trade that P&O had built up in the Mediterranean and although the war lasted less than 30 months, it was some considerable time before cruising was again considered by the company. In the meantime they continued to expand their services throughout the Indian Ocean and the Far East although this rapid expansion of ships and routes was to have its problems. For one thing the amount of coal which needed transporting to the ports where P&O ships were refuelling increased significantly. Every steamship on a trip to India needed three sailing colliers to sail ahead of it, making sure that there was enough coal for the ship to arrive at its destination. It was estimated that at any one time P&O had

over 90,000 tons of coal stored around the world ready for their ships to use on its routes to and from Britain. P&O also had to feed up to 10,000 people per day at a time when there was no frozen food or refrigeration. Ships were going to sea with entire farmyards on board, all of which would have been eaten by the time the ship arrived at its destination. To help solve this problem P&O began building its own farms on land close to the ports were the ships refuelled. This way less livestock needed to be put on the ships in Britain, meaning there was more room to carry additional cargo and a plentiful supply of suitable meat was always available once the ship had sailed.

Other shipping companies were very jealous of the success of P&O and a Parliamentary enquiry into the company was held in 1852. This found no wrongdoing by the Board of Directors and upon its completion the company celebrated its findings by winning the Royal Mail contract to Australia. The East India Company could not compete with the new and expanding company and its services to India were deteriorating as they desperately tried to hang on to their mail contracts to Bombay. They were now vastly inferior to P&O when it came to reliability, timings and comfort.

In response, the East India Company subcontracted some of its work carrying the Royal Mail and did so to less than reputable companies who on occasions lost the mail in transit. To obtain the Royal Mail run between London and Bombay it had secured subsidies from both the Indian and British Governments to the tune of over £105,000 a year at a time when P&O were waiting for the chance to outmanoeuvre the ailing company and take its trade. The opportunity came after a gross act of complacency when the East India Company managed to lose an entire consignment of Royal Mail after it had arrived at Aden where there were none of the company ships to take it on to Bombay.

Rather than wait for one of their ships to arrive, the company decided to send it on to India in an Arab dhow which left Aden and was never seen again. Upon receiving news of this debacle, the P&O board immediately submitted to the British Government a set of proposals promising to deliver the Royal Mail to India using only its large modern steamers, stopping at only British-controlled ports and for a subsidy of only one-fifth of what the Government had been paying to the East India Company. The fate of the East India Company was sealed and P&O finally won the profitable Royal Mail run to Bombay.

Matters were progressing well for P&O and the future was looking very bright when the original founder of the company, Brodie McGhie Willcox died in a freak accident just outside Portsmouth in 1862. The co-founder and driving force Arthur Anderson died a few years later in 1868. At the time of their deaths the Peninsular and Oriental Steam Navigation Company had 51 steamships in service, more than any other shipping operator, and had expanded from a simple service to the Iberian Peninsula to a large multinational company serving the British Government and carrying hundreds of thousands of passengers to three continents. In 31 short years P&O had become one of the largest and most successful shipping companies the world had ever seen.

UNDER NEW LEADERSHIP

Anderson's choice as his successor as Chairman of P&O was a young Aberdonian called Thomas Sutherland. He had joined the company when he was 18 and served at various levels on most of their trade routes. He had shown a drive and determination similar to that of Anderson himself and quickly demonstrated that he was a suitable replacement for the great man when he managed to open a new trade link to Japan when only the Dutch had been allowed to do business with what was then still a very closed and secret country. He returned to work at the company's headquarters in London and in 1872 was voted as P&O's new Managing Director at the very young age of only 38 years.

The Suez Canal had finally opened in 1869 and this caused P&O a few problems as new tonnage had to be built for the now direct service to India. The Government wanted to renegotiate its subsidiary for taking the Royal Mails as now it could be done much more efficiently and cheaply. As a result P&O saw its revenues drop at a time when its expenditures were rising; the opening of the Suez Canal was not a happy event for P&O's finances. However, the company persevered and by remaining true to its principles of offering large modern, comfortable ships, with a quick and reliable timetable, it soon overcame these adversities. This was best demonstrated in 1887 when Queen Victoria celebrated her Golden Jubilee and P&O marked the occasion by building four 6,000-ton 'Jubilee' ships, the *Victoria*, the *Britannia*, the *Oceania* and the *Arcadia*.

The company was able to make this patriotic gesture because of its success in meeting the challenge that the opening of the Suez Canal had presented. The Jubilee ships had three-cylinder, triple expansion steam engines producing 7,000 hp and turning a single propeller giving them a top speed of 16.5 knots. They had a length of 466 feet and a beam of 52 feet. Each ship cost £188,000 and was placed on the company's top links to India and Australia. The first two were built on the River Clyde by Caird & Company whilst the second two were built by Harland & Wolff in Belfast. All could carry 250 First Class and 159 Second Class passengers.

The ships were not fast like their counterparts on the North Atlantic but were broader in the beam and more comfortable in rough seas. The livery that was now adopted by P&O was a black hull, buff deck housing and black masts and funnels. The crews were generally made up of Indians in the engine room, Lascars (Indian sailors) on deck and stewards from the Portuguese colony of Goa. It has been suggested that the term 'POSH' originated from this time when influential passengers travelling to India had their tickets stamped P.O.S.H, indicating that their cabins were to be located on the portside outwards and the starboard side on the way home, thus benefiting from being on the cooler side of the ship in the afternoon whilst travelling in both directions.

THE CRUISING MARKET

By this time, the nature of P&O's trade had altered radically as revenues from the Royal Mail contracts were diminishing whilst those from passengers and cargo were increasing. In the space of 20 years the size of the fleet had increased from 80,000 tons to 200,000 tons and the run to Bombay had been reduced in time by more than a week. P&O was Britain's premier shipping company serving the Far East and very much an Imperial institution. It still had close ties with the British and Indian Governments allowing its vessels to be chartered for such uses as hospital ships and troop transports when the need was necessary. The company was doing well yet still wanted to explore ways of generating new revenue streams. It was about this time that Arthur Anderson's idea of using P&O vessels for cruising was reconsidered as other shipping companies were then beginning to advertise their own particular cruise ship services. This included the North of Scotland, Orkney and Shetland Company who began cruising to the Norwegian fjords in 1886 and the Orient Line which started cruising to the Mediterranean and Scandinavia in 1889. Both these companies had found success at an early stage and quickly turned this new industry into a handsome profit for their owners. This did not go unnoticed by P&O who would later acquire both companies. Their success gave P&O the impetus to purchase a 23-year-old ship called the *Rome* and convert her into the company's first ever real cruise ship in 1904. Built by Caird & Company in 1881, the *Rome* was just over 5,000 gross tons and her steam engines could provide around 850 horsepower giving her a top speed of around 12 knots. Renamed the *Vectis* she was more of a luxury yacht for the rich and famous rather than a cruise ship for the masses but she served the company well for eight years before being sold to the French Government in 1912.

One thing P&O had not planned for was the sudden expansion in cheap immigration travel which simply exploded at the start of the 20th century. Much has been written about this phenomena, especially the two most famous companies plying this trade across the North Atlantic, the White Star Company and the Cunard Line. Their ships had grown in size and speed in two completely different ways with one going for speed over comfort and the other going for comfort over speed. This cumulated in the ultra fast *Mauretania*, *Lusitania* and *Aquitania* being built for Cunard and the ultra luxurious *Olympic*, *Titanic* and *Britannic* being built for White Star; but for P&O the story was rather different. Up until 1910 they had concentrated all their efforts on the Royal Mail runs and the passage of wealthy First Class passengers which is why there was no Third Class on their 'Jubilee' class of ships. In 1910, P&O decided to take over the Blue Anchor Line which was a well-known, family-run business sailing between Britain and Australia around South Africa taking emigrants and cargo on the outbound journey and tea and wool on the return journey home.

It had traded well in small, efficient, if sparsely appointed vessels until 1909 when the company was struck by disaster as their newest and largest vessel, the *Waratah* disappeared without trace on a voyage back to the UK with the loss of all 211 people. The company never fully recovered from this disaster and the takeover by P&O in the following year was welcomed by many of the old employees of the Blue Anchor Line who felt that as part of the P&O empire they had a greater chance of holding onto their jobs and a more prosperous future. With the acquisition of the Blue Anchor Line, P&O could now trade at both ends of the passenger market with First Class passengers travelling to India and Australia via Suez and Third Class passengers going via the Cape.

P&O GOES TO WAR

As for Thomas Sutherland, he had now been with P&O for almost 60 years and was very close to retirement. In 1914 two major events took place that were to shape the future of P&O. Firstly P&O merged with the British India Company allowing Sutherland to retire and for the British India's Chairman, Lord Inchcape, to take control and secondly the Great War started with over 100 ships from the P&O group of companies being requisitioned by the Admirlty for military service. Within 24 hours of war being declared P&O's first requisitioning took place when the *Himalaya* was ordered to Hong Kong for fitting out with eight 4.7 inch guns. She became an armed merchant cruiser protecting trade and shipping in the China Sea. In Britain two further P&O ships, the *Mantua* and the *Macedonia* were also similarly converted and this was all in the first week of the war. Convoys started to leave India to support the British Expeditionary Force in France with over 30,000 Indian troops being moved in one convoy alone.

Considering the amount of tonnage that was lost during the Great War (around 15,000 ships sunk in all) P&O came out of it relatively unscathed. Their worse loss occurred on 30th December 1915 when the 7,974 gross tons *Persia* was torpedoed in the Mediterranean near

Top left: In this 1875 etching from The Graphic, the captain of P&O's **Sumatra** *is leading a Sunday religious service on deck as the steamer progresses through the Red Sea. (Bruce Peter collection)*

Top right: The **Himalaya** *built in 1892 was the second ship in the fleet to carry this prestigious name. (Barrow Museum)*

Above left: The first duty for the newly delivered **Medina** *was to perform the role of Royal Yacht, carrying King George V and Queen Mary to India for the Delhi Durbar in 1911. (Ambrose Greenway collection)*

Above right: The **Narkunda** *was the* **Naldera**'s *sister in the Australia service. She continued until 1942 when she was sunk by German bombers, having landed troops at Bougie in Algeria. (Bruce Peter collection)*

Crete. Nearly 500 feet long and with a beam of 53 feet, the *Persia* was powered by the highly advanced, triple expansion steam engines capable of driving the ship at over 18 knots. She was attacked by U boat *U38* at around midday whilst most of the passengers were having lunch, killing 343 of the 519 people on board. The ship had gone down with a huge fortune of gold and gems belonging to the Indian Maharaja Jagatjit Singh who had fortunately not been on the ship at the time of the sinking.

The proudest moment for P&O during the war was when Captain Archibald Smith of the *Otaki* was

posthumously awarded the Victoria Cross after his ship engaged the German surface raider *Moewe*. As a civilian, Captain Smith was not entitled to be awarded the Victoria Cross and his exploits were kept secret as it was viewed that military recognition of the defence of his ship would affect treatment of merchant prisoners of war.

The last ship lost by P&O during the conflict was the *Suranda* which was torpedoed on 2nd November, just nine days before the Armistice. In all, P&O lost around 500,000 tons of shipping throughout the Great War but due to the increase in ship building capability, managed to finish it with roughly the same amount of tonnage that it had started with.

FLEET EXPANSION

At the end of the war there was a strong rumour that P&O was about to purchase Cunard when in fact they finally bought the Orient Line and the Khedivial Mail Line. This was in addition to the Union Steamship Company which was bought in the last full year of the war. P&O's requisitions did not stop there with the General Steam Navigation Company being purchased in 1920 and Strick Line in 1923. Of the 300 plus German civilian ships that had been seized by the British Government at the end of the war, P&O bought 98 of them as passenger traffic rose sharply after the end of hostilities.

A company milestone was reached in 1923 when the *Mooltan* and the *Maloja* became the first ships ordered by P&O to be over 20,000 gross tons. A second company milestone was reached in 1924 when for the first time ever P&O recorded a profit of over £1 million. This allowed the company to go on a major spending spree where the four famous 'C' class ships were introduced. The *Cathay*, the *Comorin*, the *Chitral* and the *Corfu* were all over 15,000 tons and were powered by two four-cylinder quadruple expansion steam engines, each powering its own propeller and giving a service speed of around 16 knots. They were 547 feet long and over 70 feet wide and could carry 203 First Class and 103 Second Class passengers on the company's premier service to India and Australia. All four ships were built by Barclay Curle & Company on the River Clyde with the first two being launched on the same day by Lord Inchcape's wife and daughter.

It did not stop there with the larger and equally famous 'R' class following on with the *Rajputana*, the *Ranchi*, the *Ranpura* and the *Rawalpindi*. These were improved versions of the 'C' class and could take 307 First Class and 288 Second Class passengers. All the 'R' class ships were built at the Harland & Wolff shipyard in their lesser known yard at Greenock in Scotland and upon entry into service, were placed on the prestigious run to Bombay.

P&O's most famous ship of this time was the Royal Mail Steamship *Viceroy of India* which entered service in 1929. Originally ordered in April 1927 under the name *Taj Mahal* she was just under 20,000 tons and built by Alexander Stephen & Sons on the Clyde. She was appropriately launched on 15th September 1928 by Dorothy, Countess of Halifax, the wife of the then Viceroy of India. The 'Viceroy' was revolutionary in that she was only the third vessel in the world at that time to have turbo-electric machinery rather than steam expansion engines for her propulsion. Compared with other passenger ships in the P&O fleet at that time, the *Viceroy of India* was a fast ship, having a service speed of 19 knots

The **Chitral** *of 1925 was one of a trio of new liners completed in the mid-1920s for P&O's Australia service. (Ambrose Greenway collection)*

which allowed her to break the London to Bombay record with a time of 16 days 1 hour 42 minutes soon after entering service in September 1932. The accommodation aboard the *Viceroy of India* was truly astounding for a ship of her size, with much of it being designed by Elsie MacKay, the daughter of the P&O Chairman. She was the first P&O ship to have an indoor swimming pool and the first to have individual cabins for all of her First Class passengers. The quality of her appointments was not restricted to the higher grade passengers alone. P&O had designed the interiors of this ground-breaking vessel so that comparable advances were made in the level of comfort enjoyed by all classes throughout the ship. She was the last P&O ship to be built with the traditional black hull and black funnels for Lord Inchcape decided to paint the hulls of his next and final order of ships gleaming white with buff funnels. This was to be applied to all new P&O ships from this moment forward and is a policy that continues to this day.

This last order of Inchcape's was for five ships which were to become known as the White Sisters or the 'Straths' after the lead unit, the *Strathnaver*. She was launched on 5th February 1931 at Vickers Armstrong Ltd of Barrow in Furness by Lady Janet Bailey, second daughter of the P&O Chairman. This new ship was big by P&O's standards but much smaller than the liners on the crack North Atlantic run which by now had reached over 80,000 tons in size. The new ship was 639 feet long and 80 feet wide. She had a total gross tonnage of 22,547 tons and could carry 498 First Class passengers and 670 Tourist Class passengers as Second Class were now to be known as. She sailed on her maiden voyage from London on 2nd October 1931 to Australian via Marseilles, Suez, Bombay and Colombo. The second ship was the *Strathaird* and followed her sister into service a year later in 1932. This was a very sad year for the P&O Group as it lost its charismatic and popular Chairman, when Lord Inchcape suddenly died.

The **Strathnaver** and **Strathaird** *near completion in the fitting-out basin at Barrow-in-Furness. (Barrow Museum)*

DEPRESSION AND ANOTHER WAR

Lord Inchcape had been rewarded by the British Government for P&O's contribution to the war effort of 1914-1918 and the subsequent drive to get the British economy moving with an Earldom back in 1929.

He remained in charge of P&O until his death by which time the company was starting to feel the effects of the great depression and passenger numbers were dropping. The amount of cargo being carried had been reduced significantly and even the Royal Mail contracts could not generate the huge profits the company had seen during the previous decade.

The Chairmanship of P&O fell to Inchcape's son-in-law, the Right Honorable Lord Craigmyle who guided the company through the financial strains of the 1930s where the company forced its staff to take a 10 per cent pay cut and more often than not did not pay out any dividends to its shareholders. Despite this downturn in passenger numbers the company decided to continue with its order for the White Sisters and in 1935 Vickers Shipyard delivered the *Strathmore*, closely followed by the *Stratheden*. Both were slightly larger than the first two sisters and were instantly recognisable as they only had one funnel compared to the three of the first two ships. The fifth and final sister was the *Strathallan* which entered service in 1938 and was the last P&O ship to enter service before the outbreak of World War II. On delivery of this last ship, Lord Craigmyle retired due to ill health.

At the outbreak of hostilities, the P&O group had a total of 368 ships and just as in the First World War the company was to make a significant contribution to the British war effort. By the end of September 1939, all of the 'R' class were under Royal Navy control including the *Rawalpindi* which was requisitioned by the Admiralty on 26th August 1939 and converted to an armed merchant cruiser by the addition of eight 6 inch guns and two 3 inch guns. She was set to work from October 1939 in the Northern Patrol covering the area around Iceland. While patrolling north of the Faroe Islands on 23rd November 1939, she investigated a possible enemy sighting, only to find that she had encountered two of the most powerful German warships, the battleships *Scharnhorst* and *Gneisenau* which were conducting a sweep between Iceland and the Faroes. The *Rawalpindi* was able to signal the German ships' location back to the Home Fleet in Scapa Flow. Despite being hopelessly outgunned, the ship's 60-year-old Captain, Edward Kennedy (the father of broadcaster and author Ludovic Kennedy), decided to fight, rather than surrender as demanded by the Germans. He was heard to say, "We'll fight them both, they'll sink us, and that will be that." The German warships sank the *Rawalpindi* within 14 minutes but not before she managed to score a hit on *Scharnhorst*. A total of 238 men died when the *Rawalpindi* sank, including Captain Kennedy and 54 of the 65 P&O men still on board. Some 37 men were rescued by the German ships and a further 11 were picked up by another P&O ship, HMS *Chitral*. Captain Kennedy was posthumously Mentioned in Dispatches when clearly something like a Distinguished Service Order or even the Victoria Cross would have been more suitable.

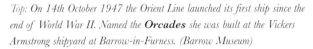

*Top: On 14th October 1947 the Orient Line launched its first ship since the end of World War II. Named the **Orcades** she was built at the Vickers Armstrong shipyard at Barrow-in-Furness. (Barrow Museum)*

*Above: The **Oronsay** served on the line's Australia run through the Suez Canal for most of her career. She became a P&O ship in 1965 before being taken out of service in 1973. (FotoFlite)*

*Right: Built for the British India Steam Navigation, the **Uganda** is pictured here passing through the Dover Strait during the early sixties. (FotoFlite)*

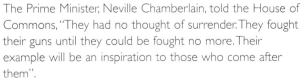

The Prime Minister, Neville Chamberlain, told the House of Commons, "They had no thought of surrender. They fought their guns until they could be fought no more. Their example will be an inspiration to those who come after them".

The loss of the *Rawalpindi* so early in the war was P&O's worst shipping disaster in the whole conflict. Other ships were lost including the *Viceroy of India* which was torpedoed on 11th November 1942 off Oran and the *Cathay* just moments later. In one operation to launch a head on the North African coast P&O lost over 110,000 tons of shipping including the almost new *Strathallan*. From the invasions of Italy to D Day and the Normandy Landings, P&O ships were in support of the Royal Navy as

*Top: As a two class ship the **Orcades** provided accommodation for 773 First Class passengers and 772 Tourist Class. In 1964 she was converted to one class for 1,635 passengers. (FotoFlite)*

*Above: Orient Line's **Orsova** arriving at Tilbury. (FotoFlite)*

either troop carriers, armoured cruise vessels or as hospital ships. They continued to support the British war effort right up to the end of hostilities in 1945 by which time they had lost 182 ships with a combined tonnage of over one million tons and over 1,000 serving crew members. World War II had taken a great toll on P&O but everyone knew that it could have been much worse.

AIR TRAVEL PROVIDES COMPETITION

P&O's headquarters in Leadenhall Street, London, had miraculously survived the Blitz so on Wednesday 18th December 1946 the company held its first post-war Annual General Meeting. The company was now lead by Sir William Currie and he outlined the future plans by stating that passenger traffic would be concentrated on the

Australia, India and China runs whilst more emphasis would be placed on its cargo business. He acknowledged that air travel would become a major player in the travel industry and that P&O should embrace this new technology and work with it rather than against it. He wanted to build new ships that were cost effective and economical to run. The company ordered its first new passenger ship, the *Himalaya* which, at a cost of £3 million, was the company's most expensive ship by some distance. The *Himalaya* was built by Vickers Armstrong in Barrow-in-Furness and had a gross tonnage of 27,955. She was also very fast with a top speed of 25 knots which would cut the UK to Bombay passage by five days and reduced the overall voyage to Australia from 38 days to just 28 days. By the time she entered service with P&O in 1949 much of the company's profile had changed and the number of cargo ships outnumbered the passenger ships by three to one.

The decline in passenger numbers meant that as older tonnage was sold off or scrapped, it was not necessarily replaced as the number of passenger ships leaving P&O far exceeded the number being built. Just a total of six new ships were built for P&O from the end of World War II to the start of the 1960s including the *Chusan* of 1950 and the second *Arcadia* in 1954. A smaller version of the *Himalaya*, the *Chusan* had a tonnage of approximately 24,215 gross tons and a capacity of just under 1,000 passengers. She was built by Vickers Armstrong in Barrow as a direct replacement for the *Viceroy of India* and was approximately 646 feet long and 85 feet wide. She was launched on 28th June 1949 and christened by the wife of Viscount Bruce of Melbourne, entering service on 1st July 1950. The new ship was extremely luxurious and well received by both her passengers and crew. One of the reasons for this was that the *Chusan* was the first passenger ship to be fitted with anti-roll stabilisers which brought a new level of comfort to her passengers that had never been experienced before. No doubt it was a result of the *Chusan*'s sea-keeping qualities that she was chosen to go on P&O's first world cruise in April 1954. The *Chusan* was also the first P&O ship to visit Japan after the end of World War II when she visited Yokohama in November 1950. She also closed the company's scheduled services to India when in January 1970 she left Southampton for the final time on a direct sailing to Bombay.

The second *Arcadia* was built by John Brown shipyards on the Clyde and was launched on 14th May 1953. She was slightly larger than the *Chusan* at 29,734 gross tons and served on the Australia run for her entire career until she was retired in 1970.

Such was the success of the new jet airliner that passenger numbers continued to dwindle and in the middle of the 1950s P&O were to order the last two ships which were to serve on any of their scheduled services. In what was a gloomy period for the company, no one ever envisaged that they would go on to have such long and successful careers and that one of them would become one of Britain's most famous and best loved ships of all time. In 1955 it was announced that two new large and extremely fast passenger ships would be delivered for the Australia service in 1960. The first would go to Orient Lines and would be called the *Oriana* whilst the second would be for P&O and in reference to the company's strong ties with Australia, would be called the *Canberra*.

NEW SHIPS FOR A NEW AGE

On 3rd November 1959, HRH Princess Alexandra launched the *Oriana* at the Vickers Armstrong shipyard at Barrow-in-Furness. She was the last ship every built for the Orient Line as the company was fully absorbed in the P&O operations in 1966 giving the corporation a new name of P&O Orient Lines. As a result, when she entered service she still wore the Orient Line traditional colour scheme of a corn-coloured hull with white superstructure and corn-coloured funnels. Her maiden voyage was from Southampton to Sydney in December 1960 and at 41,915 gross tons and a capacity for 2,000 passengers in two classes (First and Tourist), the *Oriana* was briefly the largest passenger liner in service on the UK to Australia and New Zealand route, until the introduction of the *Canberra* in May 1961. The *Canberra* had been launched by Dame Pattie Menzies, wife of the Australian Prime Minister Robert Menzies, at Harland & Wolff on 16th March 1960. She was the last passenger liner ever to be built at the famous Belfast shipyard which could pride itself on the construction of some of the biggest and most famous passenger ships of all time.

The *Canberra* was the most technically advanced ship built by P&O since the *Viceroy of India* back in 1929. All of her engineering spaces, and subsequently her funnels, were placed at the after end allowing vast open areas in the

*The first **Oriana** was built at the Vickers Armstrong yard at Barrow-in Furness and at 41,923 tonnes is the largest passenger ship ever built in England. (Barrow Museum)*

*Top: The **Canberra** was the last ocean going passenger ship built at the famous Harland and Wolff shipyard in Belfast. She is arguably P&O's most popular ship of all time and served the company for 36 years. (FotoFlite)*

*Above: The **Canberra**'s unique side by side funnel arrangement allowed for larger passenger spaces in the forward part of the ship. (Bruce Peter collection).*

*Right: The interior of the **Canberra** was designed by Sir Hugh Casson and was extremely modern and open with lots of natural light and bright colours being the predominant features. (Bruce Peter collection)*

middle of the ship to be developed as passenger areas. She was the first P&O ship to be fitted with bow thrusters to assist manoeuvring and had a real cinema on board as well as full air conditioning throughout. Arguably the single most remarkable feature of the *Canberra*'s design was her turbo-electric propulsion system. Instead of being mechanically coupled to her propeller shafts, the *Canberra*'s steam turbines drove large electric alternators which provided power to electric motors which, in turn, drove the vessel's twin propellers. They were the most powerful steam turbo-electric units ever installed in a passenger ship with around 42,500 horsepower per shaft.

All of today's modern cruise ships are powered in a similar fashion with large diesel engines replacing the *Canberra*'s steam turbines. As if this was not enough, the *Canberra* also had another feature which made her unique and set the standard for all of today's large cruise ships. Her lifeboats were placed three decks lower than usual for ships of her type and were recessed into the hull to allow improved view from the passenger decks. This was not only much safer for the passengers as in an emergency the boats did not have to be lowered right from the top of the ship but it also allowed for a huge amount of open deck space to be made available to the passengers. This

*The second P&O ship to be called the **Arcadia** was built by John Brown & Co on the Clyde and launched on 14th May 1953. She served the company until 17th February 1979. (FotoFlite)*

proved an immediate success for her mainly British passengers who have an unrivalled love of being outside when at sea.

Once the *Canberra* had entered service some of the older ships in the fleet were retired and P&O settled down with a fleet of just over 20 ships, of which most were of reasonably modern tonnage. By the mid-1960s, air transport had killed off all of the trans-Atlantic passenger traffic and was now eating into the Australian routes as well. P&O's profits were hit hard and the new chairman, Donald Forsyth Anderson, had to make some very difficult decisions which involved selling and laying off ships and of course cutting the number of people that they employed on their services. Despite the ongoing problems of the Suez Canal and the occasional mishap, including the *Oriana* colliding with an American aircraft carrier and the *Canberra* catching fire, the two ships became firm favourites of the company and were much loved by their loyal passengers.

By the start of the 1970s things were not looking too good for the company and they began to dispose of all their ships which were not making a profit or did not have a future with the company. The *Chusan*, the *Orcades* and the *Iberia* were all scrapped in the Far East, and the *Himalaya*, the *Orsova* and the *Oronsay* soon followed leaving the *Oriana*, the *Arcadia* and the *Canberra* as the

mainstay of P&O. The solution to their long-term futures was to turn these ships into one-class cruise ships and for P&O to concentrate on the holiday market as a way of returning these giants back into profitability. The P&O board saw a great future in this area of leisure, especially in the North American market where cruising was far more popular, no doubt due to the year-round hot weather in the Caribbean and the fact that the average American had more disposable income than his European counterpart. This persuaded the board to buy the successful American company of Princess Cruises in 1974 and from this point onwards the cruising arm of the P&O Group was to be known as P&O Princess Cruises.

With their change to cruising, the *Oriana* and the *Canberra* settled back into a regular routine, which would see them both based in Southampton and operating two and three-week summer cruises. The *Oriana* would spend the winter months based in Sydney with the *Arcadia* whilst the *Canberra* would start the New Year with a three-month world cruise. In 1977, the Chairman of P&O announced that the passenger division had made a £4.1 million profit in the previous trading year as opposed to a loss of £6.9 million in 1975. In 1979 the decision was taken to scrap the *Arcadia* as she was seen as being too old and outdated for any future use with the company, her place in

Sydney was taken by the *Oriana* leaving the *Canberra* as P&O's sole ship sailing out of Southampton. The *Oriana* remained in service with P&O until May 1986 when she was sold to the Daiwa House Group of Japan for conversion into a static hotel in Beppu Bay, Kyushu.

P&O AND THE FALKLANDS CONFLICT

On 1st April 1982, Argentinian forces invaded the British Falkland Islands and thus began a conflict which was going to have serious repercussions for all British merchant shipping. At the time, the *Canberra* was at the end of her world cruise and heading through the Mediterranean back to the UK. Captain Dennis Scott-Masson received a message asking for his estimated time of arrival at Gibraltar, which was something of a surprise to him as it was not on the ship's itinerary. When he called at Gibraltar, he learnt that the Ministry of Defence had requisitioned the *Canberra* so that they could use her as a troop ship and he was to immediately sail to Southampton. Other ships in the P&O fleet that were requisitioned included the educational cruise ship *Uganda*, the two ferries *Norland* and *Elk*, the tanker *Anco Charger* and a general cargo ship called the *Strathewe*.

In all, 860 crew members would remain on P&O's ships and sail to the South Atlantic with the hastily assembled 'Falklands Task Force'. After returning to Southampton the *Canberra* was modified from her cruising role into a ship more suited to her military role and sailed for the South Atlantic on 9th April, four days after the main task force lead by HMS *Hermes* and HMS *Invincible* had left Portsmouth. On board the *Canberra* were units of the Parachute Regiment and Royal Marines who were going to take part in the landings to retake the Islands. The Cunard ship *Queen Elizabeth 2* was also requisitioned but it was decided that she was too much of a national icon to be sent into a war zone which meant that the *Canberra* was going to have to do most of the dangerous work and be sent right into the heart of the conflict.

Operation Sutton was the codename for the amphibious assault to reclaim the Falkland Islands and as part of that assault the *Canberra* anchored close to San Carlos Sound just after midnight on 21st May. She went forward at around 05.20 that morning unloading her troops throughout the day and under constant attack from Argentinian aircraft. The air attacks on the ships in San Carlos Water continued until 16.00, after which time HMS *Ardent* had been sunk and HMS *Argonaut* damaged. At 19.00, the order was given to disembark the remaining troops from the *Canberra*, and at 22.42 she weighed anchor and headed out of San Carlos Water and North Falkland Sound. The *Canberra* had landed around 2,000 troops and without sustaining any real damage during the day's events. She then sailed back to Ascension Island where she picked up another set of troops from the

Queen Elizabeth 2 before sailing back to San Carlos water and again off-loading her troops in the thick of the battle. She then waited off the Islands until she was ordered back into San Carlos Sound for a third time on 15th June, this time to repatriate captured Argentinian soldiers back to South America.

Following the Argentinian surrender, the *Canberra* and the *Norland* took around 6,000 prisoners of war back to South America and after 94 days at sea, the 'Great White Whale', as the military had affectionately named the *Canberra*, returned to Southampton in what was without doubt one of the most spectacular and emotional homecomings the city had ever seen. Her Captain was awarded a CBE and made an Aide-de-Camp to Her Majesty The Queen; a very fitting tribute indeed.

After her return to civilian life and a lengthy refit, the *Canberra* returned to cruising with P&O Princess Cruises. Her role in the Falklands War made her very popular with the British public and many of her cruises were sold out months in advance. She was now Britain's most famous cruise ship and P&O started to think that the conditions were right for the company to consider ordering a brand new cruise ship, the first since the *Canberra* herself had entered service back in 1961. Before any new ship could be discussed, P&O celebrated their 150th anniversary with a lavish celebration on 7th July 1987 on board the Princess Cruises ship, *Pacific Princess* which had been moored up in Greenwich, London just for this special occasion. The highlight of the evening was a Gala dinner at which Her Majesty the Queen and the Duke of Edinburgh were the guests of honour.

Once all the euphoria of the 150th celebrations had clamed down, P&O put together a team under the name of Project Gemini to work on the new ship and after much consultation a new 69,000 gross tons cruise ship called the *Oriana* was ordered from the German shipyard of Meyer Werft in 1991.

ENTER THE NEW ORIANA

Delivered in April 1995, the new ship was named by Her Majesty the Queen in Southampton and upon entering service immediately became the largest and most expensive ship that P&O had ever owned. She was an outstanding success as demand outstripped supply with all of her cruises fully booked months in advance. When the *Canberra* was compared to the new ship it was clear that she was outdated in so many ways that it would be impossible to bring her up to the same standards. The fact that the *Canberra* was a much more fuel-thirsty vessel was the final nail in the coffin and in late 1996 it was announced that the most popular cruise ship the company had ever owned would be withdrawn from service. Her final cruise left Southampton on 10th September 1997 for a 20-night cruise around the Mediterranean, during which

*The **Seaward** was one of two ships ordered by Norwegian Caribbean Line in 1970 from the Italian shipyard of Cantieri Navali del Tirreno and Riuniti. After a dispute between the two parties the unfinished hull was sold to P&O and renamed the **Spirit of London**. (FotoFlite)*

she met up with the new *Oriana* in Cannes where passengers were able to go across in tenders for a visit on P&O's latest flagship. Later the same day, the 'Golden Cockerel', a large metal silhouette of a cockerel on a pole traditionally carried by the fastest ship in the fleet, was handed over to the *Oriana* in a ceremony eagerly watched by passengers of both ships. Upon her return to Southampton the ship de-stored before heading to Pakistani ship breakers where it took over a year to dismantle one of the last passenger ships ever built in the UK.

To replace the *Canberra* it was decided to order another brand new ship from Meyer Werft which would be even bigger than the *Oriana* and to transfer the *Star Princess* from Princess Cruises to P&O where she would become the third ship to be called the *Arcadia*. As the British cruise market continued to grow it was decided to also transfer the *Sea Princess* which would become the *Victoria* giving P&O three ships until the arrival of their new vessel after the millennium. The new ship was named *Aurora* on 27th April 2000 by Princess Anne at a lavish ceremony in Southampton before setting off on her maiden voyage on 1st May. Regrettably, this was aborted after just a few hours when a stem tube bearing overheated and failed causing the ship to return to Southampton before heading back to Germany for emergency repairs. She finally

entered service later that month with a ten-night cruise to the Canary Islands.

P&O PRINCESS CRUISES PLC AND CARNIVAL

Just before the *Aurora* entered service it was announced that all cruise ship operations were to be de-merged from the P&O group, forming a new independent company which would be known as P&O Princess Cruises PLC. This new company would also operate the other passenger shipping companies now owned by P&O including the German cruise company Aida Cruises, the river cruise company, A'Rosa Cruises and Ocean Village Cruises, a new company which was aimed at the younger and less formal market. The whole company would become independent of the P&O Group but would remain under the control of P&O's latest Chairman, Lord Sterling of Plaistow.

In April 2003 P&O Princess Cruises PLC was bought out by the American Cruise Company, Carnival Corporation, after an initial offer from rivals Royal Caribbean Cruise Lines was turned down by the P&O board. This made Carnival the world's biggest cruise operator with more cruise ships than anyone else. Apart from Carnival Cruises itself the company also owned Holland America Line, the Italian cruise company, Costa

Cruises as well as Cunard which it has purchased from Trafalgar House in 1998, meaning that the two giants of British shipping were now owned and operated by the same American company.

As soon as Carnival had completed the purchase of P&O Princess Cruises it split the company into its own individual brands which would all be controlled by the parent company from the US. This meant that P&O would now be branded as P&O Cruises with its own head office in the UK and its own set of directors which would steer the company into the 21st century.

The success of the *Oriana* and the *Aurora* was assured with record numbers of people now sailing from the UK on P&O Cruises' ships. The demand was increasing at such a significant rate that Carnival took the bold decision to transfer two of Princess Cruises' new 'Sun' class ships to P&O Cruises which at around 77,000 tonnes were similar in size and capacity to the *Aurora*. Known as 'The White Sisters', the *Ocean Princess* and the *Sea Princess* became the *Oceana* and the *Adonia* and the two vessels were renamed together in Southampton on 21st May 2003 by Princess Anne and her daughter Zara Phillips, the first double ship naming ceremony in history.

Carnival's plans for the expansion of P&O Cruises did not stop there with an announcement that they were to get a brand new ship which for the third time in less than ten years would be the biggest and most expensive ship the company had ever owned. One of the advantages of belonging to Carnival was that it brought with it a wealth of talent in cruise ship design and operation such as with the Holland America Line who since their acquisition by Carnival had three new ships built which were collectively known as the 'Vista' class. The 'Vista' class was a Panamax (Panama Canal maximum size) design of ship with a tonnage of around 85,000 tonnes and room for just over 2,000 passengers on a hull design that had a smooth and modern appearance. As the third ship in the P&O Cruises fleet to be called *Arcadia* had been transferred to Ocean Village cruising, it was decided that the new ship would become the fourth *Arcadia*. Originally ordered by Holland America Line in 2000 as their fifth 'Vista' class vessel, she was promptly transferred to Cunard Line before the keel was even laid. During the construction of the ship, Cunard decided that they wanted to bring certain attributes from their flagship, the *Queen Mary 2* to the *Queen Victoria*. However, due to her advanced stage of construction it was not possible to do this and so for the second time in her career, yard number 6078 had a change of owners and became the *Arcadia* for P&O Cruises. As a result of this, the *Arcadia* has a Cunard-style mast which is similar to those found on the RMS *Queen Elizabeth 2* and the RMS *Queen Mary 2* and a modified 'QE2' style funnel. She was launched on 26th June 2004 and entered service with the company the following April. Upon the entry into service

of the *Arcadia*, the *Adonia* was transferred back to Princess Cruises and reverted back to her original name whilst a smaller Princess Cruises ship, the *Royal Princess*, was transferred to P&O Cruises and renamed the *Artemis*.

The success of P&O Cruises continued to grow as passenger numbers sailing out of Southampton continued to increase at a substantial rate. In the last year of the 20th century fewer than 300,000 people were cruising from the Port of Southampton but, by the end of the *Arcadia*'s first year in service this number had more than doubled to over 700,000 and the number was still rising. Carnival saw the potential growth and decided that as Britain's most popular cruise line, P&O Cruises were in a good position to take advantage of this expansion so in 2006 they announced that the company was to receive the next ship of their 'Grand' class design which up until now had been exclusively for Princess Cruises, meaning that for the first time ever, P&O Cruises would have a ship of over the magic 100,000 tonnes mark.

THE 'GRAND' VENTURA AND AZURA

The 'Grand' class started life in 1997 when the *Grand Princess* entered service and briefly became the world's biggest ever cruise ship. Several sisters have followed with each being an advancement of the previous unit. The *Ventura*, as the new ship was to be known, was the tenth ship of this design and again was slightly modified from her sisters to suit the requirements of both P&O Cruises and the British cruise market. The keel was laid on 26th August 2006 and launched less than a year later. She was named by Dame Helen Mirren on 16th April 2008 before departing on her maiden voyage to the Mediterranean two days later. Even before the *Ventura* had entered service it was confirmed by P&O Cruises that the final unit of the 'Grand' class of ships was going to be assigned to them and that for the second time in two years P&O Cruises would be receiving another ship of over 100,000 tonnes. To be built at the same Italian shipyard of Monfalcone as her sister, the keel of the *Azura* was laid down on 27th October 2008 and launched on 26th June 2009 before being handed over to P&O Cruises on 1st April 2010. She was named in Southampton on 10th April by her Godmother, Darcey Bussell, a former principal dancer of the Royal Ballet. Whereas the *Ventura* had been principally designed for families with a great emphasis on children's facilities, the *Azura* was designed to appeal more to P&O Cruises' traditional client base with many of the company's familiar features (including a bar named after one of its founders) making a welcome return.

The *Azura* is as contemporary as she is large with a number of firsts for P&O Cruises, the most obvious being the open air cinema screen on the Lido Deck and the cabin accommodation for single people. She has over 900 cabins with private balconies, 11 restaurants, including

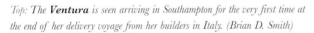

Top: The **Ventura** *is seen arriving in Southampton for the very first time at the end of her delivery voyage from her builders in Italy. (Brian D. Smith)*

Above: The **Ocean Princess** *was one of four white sisters built for Princess Cruises before being transferred to P&O Cruises in 2002 and renamed the* **Oceana**. *(P&O Cruises)*

Right: The **Azura** *was the last of the Grand Class design of ships and is a sister ship to the* **Ventura**. *(Brian D. Smith)*

signature restaurants by Atul Kochhar and a wine bar by Olly Smith, 12 bars, four swimming pools, a substantial gym, a spa, theatre, two show lounges and an open air spa terracce, exclusively for adults. She is truly worthy of being called P&O Cruises' flagship and a fantastic testament to the foresight of Brodie McGhie Willcox and Arthur Anderson. Not even they could imagine that from their humble beginnings in a small London office such a huge and impressive cruise ship capable of carrying over 3,000 people around the world would one day carry the name of a P&O Cruises flagship.

P&O Cruises has come of age with its current fleet of seven wonderful ships, including the recently introduced *Adonia* in April 2011, each with its own unique style and ambience designed to offer something for everyone in their quest for the perfect holiday. In 2011, almost 400,000

Top: The **Adonia** *was originally the eighth of a series of sister ships built for Raddison Cruises around the turn of the century. She joined P&O Cruises in April 2011 and is currently the smallest ship in the fleet. (P&O Cruises)*

Above: The **Arcadia** *is one of Carnival Corporation's successful Vista Class of ships. Laid down as the* **Queen Victoria** *she has a Cunard mast and a QE2-style funnel. (Andrew Cooke)*

people cruised with P&O Cruises on a range of cruises from a two-night party cruise to Belgium to a full world cruise lasting over 100 nights.

With the announcement that in 2015 an even larger and more impressive ship is to join the fleet, with even more new and innovative ideas to help people enjoy their time on board, it is clear that today's management have the same drive and dedication as their predecessors by investing and diversifying in an attempt to meet the challenges of running a successful cruise company in the 21st century. They are without a doubt Britain's favourite cruise company, respected and admired throughout the world for their heritage and levels of service.

Design &
Construction

The first discussions for a new *Oriana* took place in 1988 when P&O Princess Cruises were looking at the growing British cruise market. They were acutely aware that the last passenger ship the company had ordered specifically for the UK cruise market, the popular *Canberra* in 1961, was now over 25 years old and would need replacing within a decade. It was not certain whether a new ship would be a direct replacement for the much loved *Canberra* or would be a stable mate. What was clear was that any new addition to the P&O fleet would need to capture the ambience and atmosphere of this hugely successful ship. Although the company did not think the conditions were then quite right to order a new build, they wanted to put together a team of designers and engineers who, at a moment's notice, would be ready to start work on the new project. As David Dingle, the current CEO of Carnival UK said at the time, "Any large and successful cruise line should always have plans for new ships available. Opportunities to order new ships vary enormously, according to exchange rate, shipyard availability and to the financial packages on offer at any particular time." Under the project name of Gemini, a team was assembled to put to work on designing the basic requirements of the new vessel which shipyards would be invited to tender.

The P&O Chairman, Lord Sterling of Plaistow, had overall say on what was to be built and it was his insistence that the new ship must have a graceful appearance with a raked stern so that she would look appealing to the British cruise market. All the top grade cabins would have their own private balcony, more than any other cruise ship sailing out of Britain at that time, and he also suggested a large promenade deck going right around the circumference of the ship as this was something that British passengers had enjoyed since they first went to sea. There were technical requirements too for the new ship in terms of speed, sea-keeping qualities and the need for a shallower draught to increase the number of ports that the she could visit. Due to the constraints of the Panama Canal her hull could be no wider than 32.2 metres yet had to be stronger than usual to allow her to sail across the world's open oceans. For the new ship to undertake a full Mediterranean cruise and return to Southampton within a two-week period, she would need to achieve a speed of 24 knots in all but the most extreme of weather conditions.

A SWEDISH DESIGNER

Once P&O had decided on what sort of ship they

*The late Swedish architect, Robert Tillberg was responsible for the interior design of both the **Oriana** and **Aurora**. He undertook several cruises on the **Canberra** to get an idea of what a P&O ship should feel like. (Robert Tillberg Associates)*

An early rendition of what P&O Cruises' first new ship for over 30 years was going to look like. Note the curved superstructure at the front of the ship. (P&O Cruises)

wanted, they put the marketing brief for Project Gemini out to one of the company subsidiaries, Three Quays Marine Services. They would design the general arrangement and drawings for the ship which would then be sent to various shipyards for them to tender. Three Quays had an excellent marine reputation and not only worked for P&O but also shipowners and shipyards throughout the world normally seeing a shipbuilding project through from start to finish. However, with Project Gemini, they only worked up the original marketing concept to produce the general arrangement drawings, while outline specifications were prepared by another company, now under the P&O brand, called International Shipping Technical Services.

The interior design team responsible for the overall look of the ship was headed by the Swedish architect Robert Tillberg who made two trips in the *Canberra* to obtain a feel for her before he started his designs. He commented that the *Canberra* was an innovative design with her funnel and machinery placed aft to create large open passenger spaces inside while her flowing superstructure allowed for a huge amount of outside deck space which he acknowledged is a feature of any successful British cruise ship. Originally designed for the company's Australian run, the *Canberra* was built by Harland & Wolff of Belfast and entered service as a two-class ship sailing to India and Australia. By 1974 the jet aeroplane had taken just about all of the passenger traffic to Australia and so

the ship was converted to a one-class cruise vessel for just over 1,700 passengers. At one point she was P&O's only vessel in service from the UK but had built up a very large and loyal following of passengers and was much loved by the British public. P&O were very concerned that the new ship should retain the ambience and appeal of the *Canberra* and that this should be reflected in the design stage of the new ship.

THE BEST P&O TRADITIONS

When the first design was completed in September 1989, it was agreed that the ship, if possible, should be built in Britain and so the project was put to the three British

The Chairman of P&O Cruises Tim Harris and Bernard Meyer of Meyer Werft both laid lucky coins at the keel-laying ceremony of the **Oriana**. *(Meyer Werft)*

*The keel block for the **Oriana** was laid on 18th March 1993 inside the giant building hall of her German builders. Her second block is seen in the distance and was laid on the same day. (Meyer Werft)*

shipyards capable of building such a vessel. Sadly none of them could build the ship within the budget set out by P&O or guarantee the delivery date set out in the tender. This ship, although still extremely British in design and finish, would have to be built elsewhere. In total, nine European shipyards were invited to tender for the project but it was clear that under the original design she was going to be too big and too expensive for P&O's projected needs and of the shipyards that actually tendered for the project, only Meyer Werft in Germany and Kvaerner Masa

An aerial view of the Meyer Werft shipyard which is situated on the River Ems close to the Dutch border. (Meyer Werft)

(now STX) of Finland could meet the desired delivery date. It was decided to put the whole project on hold for another two years to see if the conditions for ordering a new ship would improve.

In the summer of 1991, the number of British people embarking on a cruise was increasing by about 15 per cent per year at a time when the British pound was extremely strong against European currencies meaning that the price of a new ship was now very favourable. The two shipyards that P&O now wanted to build the ship were invited to re-tender but yet again the original design for Project Gemini was still too large and too expensive for P&O's needs. To solve the problem it was decided to put out a new marketing brief based on the original designs to both shipyards and to let them submit their own general arrangements at a price that P&O could afford. Kvaerner Masa came up with a ship which was too small for P&O's needs, however, Meyer Werft designed a ship which the P&O board liked the sound of. It was 260 metres in length, around 69,000 gross tons in size and would carry just over 1,800 passengers on ten decks. Meyer Werft concentrated on the lower decks of the ship where all the engineering and machinery would be situated whilst the P&O team worked on the upper decks and the passenger areas. The result was a ship that was just perfect for P&O and could

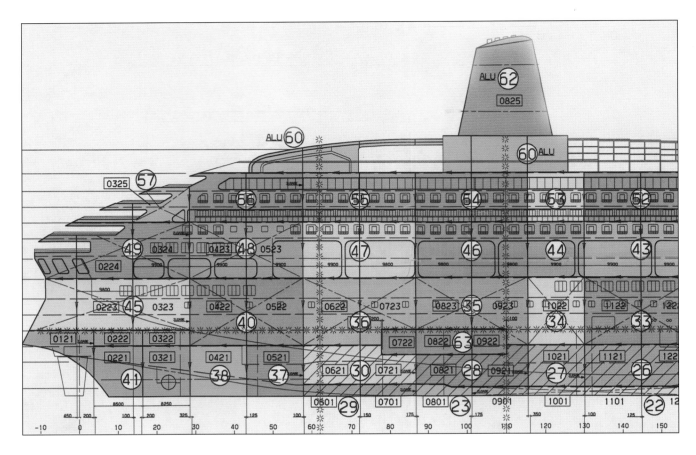

Each ship is built to the block principle with each numbered block being constructed in time to be added to the next. Here we see the rear section of the **Aurora***'s block diagram.*

be built on time and within budget in Germany. It was also to be the largest ship ever ordered by P&O or built by Meyer Werft.

CONTRACT SIGNED

The contract was signed in December 1991 at a cost of £200 million and announced to the world on 20th January 1992, the 84th birthday of Joseph Franz Meyer, the oldest member of the founder family of Meyer Werft still alive. The project manager was the former Royal Navy Commander and engineer, Jim Hunter who worked with the design architects and the yard's naval architects to finalise the drawings and specification that the ship would be built to. P&O had invited many British concerns to tender for work on the new vessel and contracts were signed with over 50 UK-based companies. The new ship would have 17 public rooms, more than any other cruise ship at that time, and a greater range of cabin accommodation to appeal to all sections of the British cruise market. She would have the largest swimming pool ever built for a cruise ship and more outside deck space than anything else afloat. The *Canberra* theme was to be continued with open bridge wings, a pub with a cricket theme, angled stiffeners between the lifeboats and a funnel

which would be designed to look like the distinct twin arrangement on the Belfast ship.

Before any construction of the *Oriana* could begin, two models of the design were made and tested in an experimental model tank in the Norwegian town of Trondheim. The models were tested in up to Force 10 conditions which allowed for the optimum design for the ship's hull that had the minimum resistance for the required speed. Sea keeping is a compromise between speed and stability and these tests allowed for the best design to be calculated for the required specification. Having finished the tank tests, the models were moved to Vienna for further aerodynamic tests in wind tunnels. Tests on model propellers and rudders were also carried out as well as studies into noise and vibration reduction. Almost a year after the contract was signed, the final design was approved and the first steel was ready to be cut. This was carried out at a special ceremony at the shipyard in October 1992.

WORLD'S LARGEST INDOOR DRY DOCK

The *Oriana* would not be built in the open air on a traditional slipway, as most people imagine a ship to be built, but inside Meyer Werft's giant ship building hall which

*The lifting cranes at Meyer Werft can lift up to six hundred tonnes at a time. Here we see them positioning one of the front blocks of the **Oriana** into place. Note the P&O insignia. (Meyer Werft)*

building methods to the modular block construction method. This involves steel being formed into large separately numbered blocks which are then lowered into the building dock and welded together. These blocks can be anything up to four decks high and weigh up to 600 tonnes, which was the maximum lifting weight of Meyer Werft's internal cranes. They house all the piping, electrical ways and access areas required in building a new ship. One

block is built onto another block until the hull of the ship is complete which is a much faster and more efficient way to build large passenger ships. The more immense components of the construction process such as the engines and generators are loaded onto the finished blocks inside the building dock. In many ways it is like building a ship to the Lego principle.

The *Oriana* would have 45 prefabricated blocks made

*The outline of the steelwork is easily recognisable as the **Oriana** by the angled lifeboat stiffeners which were purposely designed in reverence to the popular **Canberra**. (Meyer Werft)*

up during her construction. The largest of these would be block 16 which at 722 tonnes had to be built in two parts and would house the ship's engines. The total amount of steel used in the *Oriana*'s construction was 14,830 tonnes. It is worth mentioning here that the ship's gross tonnage does not bear any relation to the weight of steel in her construction. Gross tonnage is a measure of internal capacity which is measured by taking the total enclosed volume of the ship in cubic feet and dividing this number by 100; thus one gross ton equals 100 cubic feet. Therefore the *Oriana* has a total capacity of 6,915,300 cubic feet or 69,153 gross tons.

On 11th March 1993 the official keel-laying ceremony took place at the bottom of the giant dry dock where the new ship was to be built. Tim Harris, the Chairman of the cruise division of P&O placed a newly minted one penny piece onto of the blocks that were to support the new ship whilst Bernard Meyer, the Managing Director of Meyer Werft and a direct descendent of the shipyard's founder Willm Rolf Meyer, placed a German pfennig. During the speeches Tim Harris confirmed for the first time that the ship would be called the *Oriana*. She was to be the second P&O Cruises ship to carry the name, the first being built for the Orient Line and in service from 1959 until 1986. After a lengthy campaign, P&O were permitted to allocate the new *Oriana* the call sign GVSN which was the same call sign as her predecessor. Once the speeches were finished the first steel block was lowered down onto the coins and the construction was officially under way. A formal lunch then took place with over 100 guests being invited from the media and travel trade. After the lunch the second part of the keel-laying service took place with the next building block being lowered onto of the first. Within four months over 4,000 tonnes of steel had been used in the construction and the superstructure had reached up to Deck 10.

THE ENGINES

At the early assembly phase of a new ship comes some of the most complex and intricate parts of the construction process, including the installation of the engines and propulsion systems. The engines themselves are not manufactured by the shipyard but are built to order by a chosen manufacturer. The *Oriana*'s engines were built by the German company M.A.N, at their main factory in Augsburg, who at the time were known as M.A.N B&W after the company took over the Danish engine manufacturer Burmeister & Wain in 1980. They also bought the British engine companies of English Electric, Mirrlees Blackstone, Napier & Son, Paxman, and Rustons.

*Left: By the beginning of 1994 the lower hull of the **Oriana** was complete with just a few additional building blocks needed to complete the passenger superstructure. (Ferry Publications Library)*

*An interesting view of the **Oriana** looking through her partially completed decks from the tank top to deck nine. Her starboard stabiliser is being lowered into position. (Meyer Werft)*

*The **Oriana** is waiting to be floated out of her building hall for one day on 30th July 1994 to perform the preliminary incline test to help ascertain the ship's centre of gravity. (Mike O'Dwyer)*

M.A.N are famous for the work they did with Dr Rudolf Diesel in the late 1890s producing the world's first diesel engine. Today their engines are manufactured in Germany, Denmark and France as well as under licence to selected manufacturers around the world. Almost every new cruise ship built today will have engines from M.A.N or the Finnish company, Wartsila. The number of engine manufacturers who are capable of building such engines are extremely limited and at one point it was a major concern to the shipyards of the world as ships were being constructed faster than the engines to power them were being built. Once constructed, the engines are delivered to the shipyard exactly in time to be installed into the hull. Such engines, being far too big and heavy for road transport, are transported by sea. In the case of the *Oriana* they were sailed up the River Ems to the shipyard where they were carefully craned off the transport barges and moved into the building hall. Once inside, the hall's giant overhead cranes gently positioned each engine into the ship's hull. The placement of each engine directly onto its respective bed is a mixture of the exceptional power of the cranes combined with the gentle touch of the human hand to help guide it into position.

*The bow of the **Oriana** starts to take shape as the passenger accommodation grows to Deck 10 in the background. (Meyer Werft)*

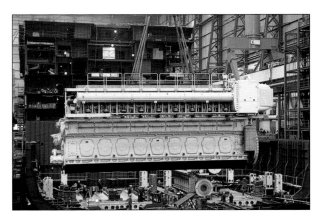

*One of the **Oriana**'s huge 9 cylinder M.A.N. diesel engines which weigh 211 tonnes is lowered into the hull of the ship. (Meyer Werft)*

*The **Oriana** leaves her building hall for the last time on 7th January 1995. Her lifeboats would be added to the ship once she had completed her River Ems passage. (Meyer Werft)*

FATHER AND SON

The design team for the *Oriana* had chosen to opt for a traditional engine and gearbox arrangement, known as direct drive. This meant that the ship had eight large M.A.N B&W four stroke diesel engines producing a total of 57,430kW or 78,100 horsepower. Four of the engines are for propulsion and four for the ship's electrical requirements. The propulsion engines are arranged in pairs, each consisting of a nine-cylinder and a six-cylinder engine.

The smaller engine is arranged outside of the larger engine in what is commonly known as a father and son configuration. Each of the larger engines weighs 211 tonnes and develops 11,925kW at 428 revolutions per minute (rpm). To give an idea of scale, a typical family car diesel engine produces 100kW at around 4,000 rpm. The smaller engines weigh 149 tonnes and produce 7,950kW at exactly the same rpm. This gives the *Oriana* a total shaft propulsion power of 39,750kW. This power is transmitted to the propellers through two giant gearboxes, each weighing 106 tonnes.

Both gearboxes were made by a sister company of M.A.N called Renk Tacke and are designed to be as silent as possible. Despite their enormous size, they are calibrated to a very fine tolerance and are insensitive to the movement of the ship or different loads from the engines. They reduce the engine speed down to the propeller speed of 128 rpm. The gearboxes have an interesting feature in that each also drives a generator able to produce electrical power for the on-board services. The four other engines that power the independent generators for the electrical supply create around 17,600kW of electrical power. Again to give some idea of scale, this is exactly the same as the total engine output of a large cross-Channel ferry seen sailing out of Dover to Calais.

The marine diesel engine is very fuel efficient; however, as almost a third of the entire diesel burned in an engine is emitted as heat, it is important to try and capture this and to use its energy as efficiently as possible. Inside the engines' exhaust system is a boiler unit which works on the exhaust gas recovery system. Hot gases from the engines are recycled through a heat exchange mechanism which heats up water before it can then be used throughout the ship. The boiler plant for the *Oriana* was designed and built by Senior Thermal Engineering of Wakefield in Yorkshire. The system has a total of six boilers which extract the heat at different points in the exhaust process right up until the point it is emitted from the funnel. This allows for the maximum amount of heat to be recovered, making the whole process very efficient.

WHEELS, STABILISERS AND JOYSTICKS

The technical team elected to use shaft propellers and rudders and not the new and evolutionary Azipod podded propulsion system. Although Azipods do offer smoother running and greater manoeuvrability, they are very expensive to build and maintain and were an unproven technology in 1992. The *Oriana*'s two propellers are manufactured by the Dutch company L.I.P.S and made of Cunial, a mixture of copper, nickel and aluminium. Each weighs 32 tonnes and has four 5.8-metre wide blades. They are variable pitched which means the engines never go into reverse. The *Oriana* has three bow thrusters and one stern thruster to assist with manoeuvring. The whole propulsion system is operated by one joystick on the bridge, through the 'Lipstronic' computerised control system. This single lever co-ordinates the propellers, thrusters and rudders to work in one single operation.

The *Oriana* needed to be as stable as possible when sailing in heavy seas, so the ship was fitted with the largest set of stabilisers ever fitted to a passenger ship at that time. Stabilisers look like small aeroplane wings and extend out from the ship's hull just a few feet under the surface of the water and are retracted when not required or when the ship is docking. Made by Brown Brothers of Edinburgh,

in the construction project are the huge salt water evaporators which supply enough fresh water for her everyday needs. These are two steam-heated, multi-stage flash evaporators which basically heat the seawater, collecting the evaporation and cooling it before distilling, filtering and disinfecting it so that it can be drank safely. These can turn around 9,000,000 litres of seawater into around 600,000 litres of drinking water every day. Although not particularly efficient, the plant was one of the most modern and up-to-date units ever seen on a passenger ship. This was one of the last major engineering components installed in the lower decks before the vast areas of passenger decks could be built on top.

The shipyard continued to manufacture the remainder of the large steel blocks that would house the passenger accommodation, including the bridge, and lift them onto the ship as the testing and commissioning of the engineering equipment got under way. At Meyer Werft it is customary to complete the bow section of the ship before

*The **Oriana**'s funnel waits on the quayside for the ship to be undocked from Meyer's building hall, it being too big to be fitted inside. (Meyer Werft)*

*As the stern of the **Oriana** slowly moves out of the building dock, the funnel is raised into position by two of the yard's outside cranes. (Meyer Werft)*

The out docking is halted for a few minutes for the giant chimney pot to be lowered into position. (Meyer Werft)

they have a surface area of 21.5 square metres and weigh 93 tonnes each. They are computer controlled and are tilted automatically as the ship begins to roll. The size of these fins eliminated the need for a second set of stabilisers which would have been more expensive and increased fuel consumption.

GLASS WALLS, STEEL BLOCKS AND PAINTING

Most of the engineering side of the ship, which is to do with the propulsion systems, is installed in the hull before any of the passenger accommodation is added. Other technical equipment such as the air conditioning units, the hot water systems and the heating components are added as the ship grows. By the end of 1993, the lower sections were completed and the job of commissioning the engines and propulsion systems could then begin. Another interesting feature which is built into the ship at this point

the stern as there is less technical installation in this area at this stage of construction. Almost on a weekly basis another of the huge steel blocks that made up the *Oriana* was added to the hull and slowly but carefully the bare metal work, which until this time had simply looked like a housing for a collection of very large machinery, started to take on the form of a wonderfully graceful passenger ship. All it needed now was painting and it would not be very hard to imagine what the finished result would look like once she was completed and was sailing on the open sea.

As the steel work reached the upper decks, it became noticeable that there were no windows in the topmost passenger decks but large gaping holes that ran the full length of the ship. The reason for this was that the upper passenger decks were to be given a feature which had never been previously seen on a British cruise ship. All the outer walls on the upper decks of the ship were not made of the customary steel but glass. This was achieved by building extremely large glass panels which are over seven feet tall and held in place with thin metal struts directly attached to the ship's superstructure allowing passengers unprecedented panoramic views that a normal window simply could not give. The technology to construct this sort of feature was not available on any previous British passenger ship and was another new and innovative characteristic of the *Oriana*.

By July 1994 most of the hull and superstructure had been completed and the task of painting the giant colossus could now begin. The ship was, of course, painted in white with the exception of the funnel which would be the traditional P&O buff yellow. The type of paint used is a special type designed to improve the gloss and colour retention called Interthane cover coat which is manufactured in the UK by International Marine Coatings. They also provided another type of special paint used on the underwater parts of the ship. Called Intershield, it provides protection from abrasion and corrosion, minimising future maintenance costs for the rest of the ship's life. There are over 100,000 litres of paint on the hull of the *Oriana*. Whilst all this painting was going on, the last piece of steel to be fitted to the ship's hull, the bulbous bow, which protrudes from under the ship's stem below the surface of the water and greatly improves the ships hydrodynamics and therefore fuel consumption, was welded into place. This meant that the hull was now

complete and everyone could turn their attention to the completion of the passenger accommodation ready for the ships delivery in April.

FLOATING UP

An important milestone in the construction of any new ship is when she floats in water for the first time and for the *Oriana* this landmark was reached on 27th July 1994. The huge dry dock in which the ship was sitting was cleared of all building material and the ship's hull thoroughly checked to make sure that there were no obvious defects and that she was completely sound and ready to take to the water. Once this was completed, a special ceremony was held in front of invited guests to mark the occasion before a button was pushed which opened the dock's giant sluice gates allowing millions of litres of seawater to pour into the dry dock where the ship had been constructed. It is a far simpler and safer way of launching large ships than the more traditional method of sliding a new hull into the water by way of an angled slope. After about six hours there was enough water for the *Oriana* to float and as the amount of water in the dock equalled the weight of the ship, she gently lifted off her construction blocks and was afloat for the very first time. Immediately, shipyard workers re-entered the hull to check for leaks or any other defects which could compromise the ship's safety.

*With the funnel in position the graceful lines of the **Oriana** can be appreciated for the first time. (Meyer Werft)*

Seen at the outfitting dock of her builders, the **Oriana** *spends her last night at the place of her birth. (Meyer Werft)*

Once satisfied that the hull was sound and there was enough water in the dock to support the ship, the sluice gates were closed and the *Oriana* sat proudly afloat inside the giant hall where she was built. Three days later, she was slowly moved out of her construction hall so that a small incline test could be performed and her builders could confirm that her centre of gravity was exactly where it should be. Once this was completed, several other minor tests were carried out before she was pulled back into the hall to allow for her final commissioning.

Before the hull of the *Oriana* was even complete, work was being carried out to fit out the miles of piping and electrical wiring that a modern cruise ship requires. Meyer Werft has its own pipe manufacturing plant on site and all the piping on the *Oriana* was built and installed by employees of the yard. When one considers the needs of the kitchen galleys, the swimming pools, the laundries, the bars and all the cabins, it can be seen what a mammoth task is involved to connect all the services safely around the ship. The water on board needs to be kept fresh and the waste properly treated before being retained or pumped into the sea although no untreated water is discharged into the sea as the *Oriana* is a very environmentally friendly ship. There are four large sewage

treatment plants which were made by Hamworthy Engineering in Dorset and are more than capable of dealing with the daily requirements of the 2,800 people who will be on board at any one time. They operate on the extended aeration principle, which accelerates nature's biological process to purify the 'black water' as it is known on a ship.

CABINS FROM BRITAIN

The *Oriana* was to have 914 passenger cabins which, with double occupancy, would set her optimum passenger capacity to 1,828. However, her maximum capacity was set at 1,975, allowing for multiple occupancy of some cabins. Each cabin is built as a separate individual module at the shipyard which contains the living area and a bathroom (known as the wet area). Once each module is complete it is moved to the construction hall then lifted into a gap which has been deliberately left in the side of the ship's hull and placed in a pre-arranged position ready to be connected to the ship's services such as the electrical and water supplies. When all the cabins are installed, the gap is plated up and the cabins are later fitted out with all the soft furnishings such as the bed lining, the carpets and curtains and the occasional furniture. Once this is done the

*The **Oriana**'s journey down the River Ems from Papenburg to the North Sea had to be done in two stages as she could only be moved on a high tide. Here she waits for the next high tide at the market town of Leer. (Meyer Werft)*

cabin is then sealed and waits for an acceptance check from the owner. The cabin furnishings on the *Oriana* were crafted by Englender's of Derbyshire to the specifications set out by the cabin designer, Petter Yran meaning that each piece of furniture was hand built to the design for the particular cabin it was going into. Between November 1994 and January 1995 the company sent over 70 containers full of furniture to be installed on the *Oriana*. This created a real logistical challenge as each dispatch had to be labelled by cabin grade as there were over 90 different design or fabric variations in addition to over

1,000 settees which needed re-assembling on arrival at the shipyard. P&O had several cabin mock-ups completed as early as July 1992 which were assessed by past passengers, members of the travel trade and stewards from the company's other ships who made several recommendations before an optimal design was agreed upon.

As the passenger cabins were being fitted, work continued on the other passenger spaces around the ship such as the installation of the carpets in the public rooms and stair cases which were all manufactured by the British

*A large modern cruise liner is not something you expect to see in rural North Germany but here the **Oriana** looks quite at home amongst the local wildlife on the second part of her River Ems passage. (Meyer Werft)*

*The skill needed to guide the **Oriana** through the tight turns of the River Ems can be appreciated in this ariel photograph of the ship as she waits to sail through the Jann Berghaus road bridge in Leer. (Meyer Werft)*

company, Brintons of Kidderminster. In total they supplied 47,840 square yards of carpet, ranging from the alternating light and dark green shades replicating a cricket pitch in the Lord's Tavern pub to the Tudor roses adorning the floor of the gentlemen's club called Anderson's after one of P&O's founders, Arthur Anderson. Brintons are experts in designing and fitting carpets to passenger ships as they have supplied carpets and furnishings to over 250 vessels and currently have a very full order book with various cruise companies across the world. The furniture for the two restaurants was installed, including 86,546 pieces of china, designed jointly by one of the *Oriana*'s principal architects, John McNeece, and one of Britain's most famous companies, Wedgwood. It all featured the historic rising sun motif which was the same as the emblem on the bow of the ship and which is now used by P&O Cruises.

The four-deck waterfall in the *Oriana*'s atrium is over 15 metres high and was installed by Rochester-based Watermark Hydronamics. The first of its kind at sea, it is a masterpiece of design with the whole effect created by tiny rivulets of water running down the fine glass threads to a small pond in front of the main reception desk before being pumped back up to the top and used again. By September the galleys for the restaurants were being completed and the theatre was being installed with a unique air conditioning system which allowed air to be pumped direct to every one of the theatre's 650 seats. It was also fitted out with the latest technology to allow the P&O production teams to put on lavish West End style shows.

By the start of 1995 the three swimming pools, including the Crystal Pool which at just under 13 metres long was the longest swimming pool ever installed on a passenger ship, had been tiled and the beautiful teak wood laid on the promenade deck which went around the entire circumference of Deck 7. A bronze water sculpture by Andre Wallace featuring a rower and a sunbather had been placed on the pool deck overlooking the Crystal pool and over 3,000 pieces of works of art that had been especially commissioned by P&O for the new ship hung in the cabins and public areas. These had been shipped from Britain by Momart, who had also packed pictures for the Tate Gallery in London. Like the cabins, they were also shipped by P&O Containers, on a P&O ferry in a P&O trailer. Other sculptures, such as the two of Charlie Chaplin for the cinema and the Indian elephants in the Curzon Room, were installed alongside other works by John Mills and Robert Erksine to name but two. The deep leather chairs in Anderson's Bar were delivered alongside all the other soft furnishings for the Pacific Lounge and the other bars and public areas of the ship. Every day another part of the ship was completed and the *Oriana* looked less and less like a building site and more and more like the beautiful cruise ship that she was to become.

SEA TRIALS

On the technical side, the bridge navigational equipment was all fitted and the initial commissioning of the main and auxiliary machinery was completed. The propellers and rudders had been fitted and tested in situ; nothing much else could be done until the *Oriana* was removed from her building hall. In early January 1995, Meyer Werft finally announced that the great ship was ready to leave the shipyard and make her way to the open sea for further trials. So for a second and final time she was moved out of the hall and was fitted with her funnel which was waiting on the quay just outside as the superstructure was too large to have it fitted inside. The shape of the funnel is always the subject of careful design and testing as apart from contributing to the distinctive appearance of the ship, it is very important that the exhaust gases from the engines do not fall onto the open deck spaces and are emitted in the most environmentally friendly way as is possible. These studies are performed in a wind tunnel where the so-called 'comfort test' is performed which allows the optimisation of not just the funnel but also the upper passenger deck spaces in order to prevent the flow of wind over the open decks becoming too strong and uncomfortable for the passengers. The ship was then positioned at the fitting-out berth where over the next few days she was prepared for her one and only departure from Meyer Werft, her passage down the River Ems to the North Sea and her eventual sea trials.

As Papenburg is situated some 26 miles from the sea and the River Ems is both shallow and narrow, the *Oriana*'s first journey was at a very slow speed of around three knots taking almost 24 hours to complete as she could only be moved at high water. On her journey she passed through the Friesenbrucke railway bridge at Weener where a whole section of the bridge was dismantled to allow the *Oriana* to pass through. This obstacle was followed by the Jann Berghaus road bridge at Leer where a bascule lift bridge was raised giving unlimited clearance for the new ship. She also passed over the A31 motorway, which runs under the River Ems via two large tunnels, giving motorists a grandstand view as they drove beneath her.

To be sure of success, the ship's draught was reduced from 7.9 metres to 7.3 metres by removing all the lifeboats and pumping out all unnecessary oil and water that she did not need. This 'conveyance' (as the shipyard like to call this river transit) always attracts many people to see this extraordinary spectacle that has become a major tourist attraction for Meyer Werft's home town of Papenburg. All of the hotels are fully booked within days of the event being advertised and many visitors camp out or park up in motor homes at the best viewing spots to watch the ship sail down the river. The 'conveyance' was not conducted by the *Oriana*'s crew, as the ship had not yet been accepted

*During her sea trials in the North Sea the **Oriana**'s sea-keeping qualities were severely tested when she encountered winds in excess of Force 9 on the Beaufort Scale. She proved herself to be a very steady ship in all weathers. (Ferry Publications Library)*

Artist Janet Shearer visited Lord's to watch several cricket matches before creating a large mural. (Ferry Publications Library)

Sculptor John Mills at work in his studio on one of the sculptures for Harlequins. (Ferry Publications Library)

Sarah Janson sketching for one of her Trompe l'oeil paintings. (Ferry Publications Library)

by P&O and still belonged to Meyer Werft, but by the Pilots' Association of Emden who have not only carried out many of these river passages previously but have been training for months in a simulator ready for this event. Early on Sunday 26th February 1995, the *Oriana* left Papenburg and completed the first 13 miles of her passage before stopping overnight at the market town of Leer. At the narrowest point on the journey, the 32-metre wide ship had to pass between two bridge supports on the old railway bridge at Weener which were only 47 metres wide. Power cables across the river had to be tautened to provide an additional nine inches of clearance, yet still the hull was only six inches from the bottom of the river. After her night stopover, the *Oriana* recommenced her journey on the following day's high tide.

After the completion of her 'conveyance', the *Oriana* was based in the German port of Emden for her two sets of sea trials. The first are the builder's trials where Meyer Werft test the ship to the limit by carrying out such manoeuvres as crash stops from full speed, using the stabilisers in reverse to induce roll and taking the ship on minimum turning circles. After these are completed the owner's acceptance trials are done where P&O makes sure that the ship does everything that it is supposed to do in

the contract. Of particular importance was the requirement for the ship to sail at 24 knots as anything less and the ship would not be able to meet her planned sailing schedule. These tests were carried out in the North Sea where the wind never dropped below Force 7 on the Beaufort scale. The trials also provided an opportunity for any sources of vibration and unnecessary noise to be identified and corrected. It was during these trials that excessive cavitations (vibrations) were noted coming from the ship's propellers that would delay her eventual handing over to P&O. The problem was resolved in a most straightforward and ingenious way with the engineers simply reversing the direction that the propellers turned. Other minor mechanical matters also had to be re-addressed as a result of this but basically the cause of the problem was identified and the ship could now be handed over to P&O, a day or two later than planned.

SOUTHAMPTON ARRIVAL

The *Oriana* was delivered to her new owners on Friday 2nd April 1995 and to mark the occasion a ceremony was held on board the stern of the ship where the Meyer Werft flag was lowered and the P&O house flag raised in its place. In addition, the Red Ensign was proudly

Alice Kettle created an ambitious series of embroideries for the Curzon room. (Ferry Publications Library)

The entrance to the Chaplin's cinema. (Ferry Publications Library)

Petter Yran's choice of fabrics for the cabins was crucial for the overall feel of the vessel. (Ferry Publications Library)

At speed in the English Channel the first ship ever built for the British cruise industry makes for a magnificent sight and every bit what a modern British cruise liner should look like. (FotoFlite)

*The **Aurora** was built in the same building hall as the **Oriana** but in a much shorter time frame. (Meyer Werft)*

*In the Medina Restaurant, **Aurora**'s passengers could make a grand entrance on the double staircase entrance from the deck above. (Meyer Werft)*

The first fitting of the Alexandra Restaurant shows some of the pipework needed to supply all of the services on a modern cruise ship. (Meyer Werft)

flown as she was formally handed over to Lord Sterling by Bernard Meyer. Once the festivities were completed the ship, now officially a P&O cruise ship, sailed direct to Southampton arriving early on the morning of 4th April. In view of her slightly delayed arrival, matters now had to be rushed to have the *Oriana* ready for her naming ceremony which was to be performed by Her Majesty the Queen. A dedicated inaugural team spent thousands of hours planning everything from the seating positions of the guests to the music played by the Royal Marines' Band.

On 6th April, at 11.20 precisely, HM The Queen and HRH The Duke of Edinburgh arrived in Southampton Docks on board the Royal Train. They were welcomed by the Lord Lieutenant of Hampshire, Mrs Mary Fagin and Lord and Lady Sterling escorted them past a guard of honour formed by members of the *Oriana*'s Pakistani crew in full ceremonial uniform. They then made their way to the specially constructed dais where other distinguished guests were waiting. The music for the occasion included the Elizabethan madrigal, 'Fair Oriana' and 'Fanfare for Oriana'. Before the prayers and blessing were pronounced by The Right Reverend Dr Geoffrey Powell, Bishop of Basingstoke, the choir of Westminster Abbey sang Vaughan

Williams' anthem, 'O Clap Your Hands'. There then followed the sailors' hymn, 'Eternal Father, Strong to Save'. Once these had finished, the Queen welcomed the *Oriana* as very much a British ship which was British owned and British registered flying the Red Ensign proudly from her stern. She mentioned that Britain had not lost touch with its maritime heritage and commented on the Royal Family's links with P&O which went right back to 1840 when Queen Victoria first gave the company its Royal Charter to carry the Royal Mail. Then, just before midday came the moment everyone had been waiting for as the Queen said those magical words, "I name this ship *Oriana*. May God bless her, and all that sail in her." She then pressed a button which released a magnum of champagne against the ship's hull and the P&O fanfare was then sounded in celebration. The Royal Party then boarded the newly christened ship for a private luncheon and tour. As the festivities were coming to a close, Lord Sterling presented the *Oriana*'s Captain, Ian Gibb with a replica of a P&O Officers' Sword, a traditional gift on the occasion of a visit by a reigning monarch.

On 9th April, after a couple of days of being shown to the press and travel trade, the *Oriana* set off on her

*One of the **Aurora**'s main propulsion engines is offloaded from its delivery barge and carefully transported to the building hall. (Meyer Werft)*

*Unlike the **Oriana**, the **Aurora**'s propellers are five bladed instead of four but are fixed pitch as the electric motors control the speed and direction of the shaft. (Meyer Werft)*

*The bridge of the **Aurora** before the installation of her highly sophisticated navigational equipment. (Meyer Werft)*

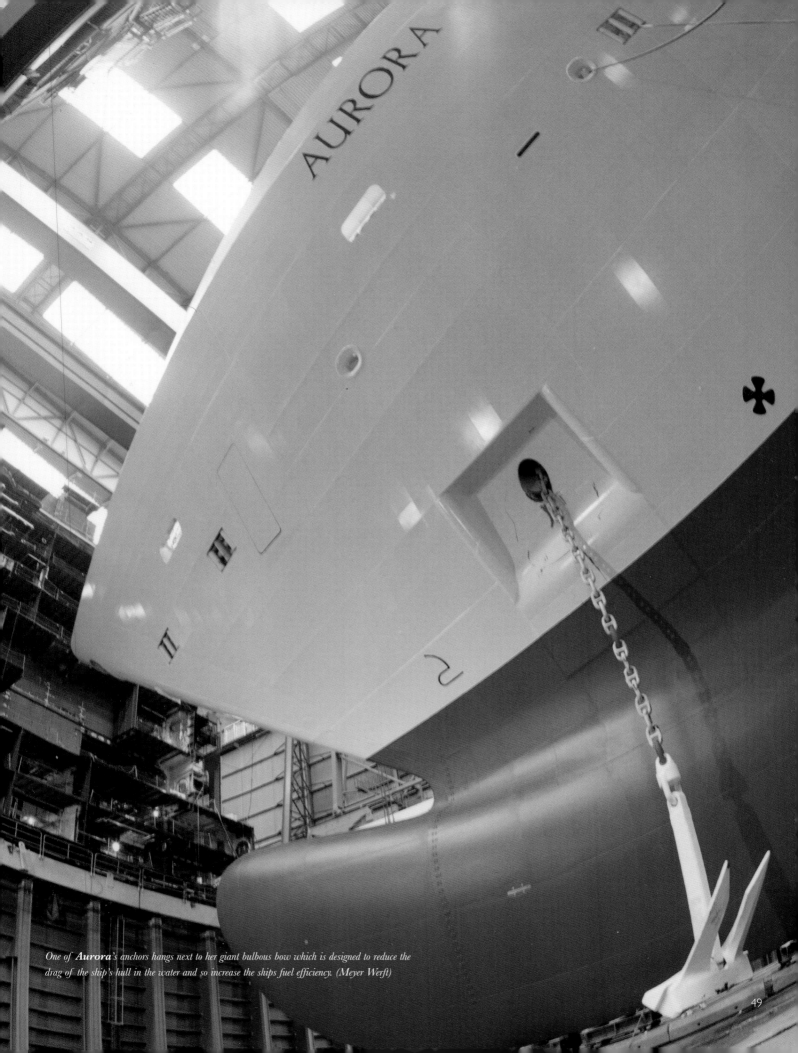

*One of **Aurora**'s anchors hangs next to her giant bulbous bow which is designed to reduce the drag of the ship's hull in the water and so increase the ships fuel efficiency. (Meyer Werft)*

Maiden Voyage to the Canary Islands. She was immediately a great success and numbers travelling with P&O increased significantly as the new ship generated her own trade. Everyone loved the ship and wanted to be among the first to travel on her. It was clear that the numbers of passengers wishing to travel from the UK were increasing and future predictions showed this would continue well into the 21st century. The P&O board were delighted with the public response to the ship and at a meeting in late 1996 it was agreed to order a second vessel based on the success of the *Oriana* but to incorporate improvements to make the new ship even more thrilling. Project Gemini became Project Capricorn and the dawning of the *Aurora* had begun.

PROJECT CAPRICORN

Several things had changed at the P&O Group since Project Gemini had first been discussed nine years earlier. One of the most important matters which would involve future new builds was the acquisition of the American cruise company, Sitmar International Cruise Operations. This company had four ships in service and were major competitors to P&O's sister company, Princess Cruises. However, the real reason that Lord Sterling had gone for the company was the fact it had three very large cruise ships under construction and the price quoted for the new company was just £125 million which was basically less than the cost of one new ship. For a very modest price, P&O Princess Cruises now had three of the world's newest and largest cruise ships under its ownership. What they also acquired was a team of experts who were at the technological front of new cruise ship design and although this team worked on the new *Oriana*, they arrived too late to make any changes to the drawings put forward by the original design team.

As Project Capricorn was to be an evolvement of the *Oriana*, additional funds were made available to the design team in an endeavour to bring the best elements of cruise ship innovation to the project, whilst still retaining the essence of P&O's classic traditions. Tillberg Design was again chosen as co-ordinating architects, this time with Anders Johansson taking most of the design leads, including a charge with streamlining the external profile of the ship. He was to work with a subsidiary called SMC Design as well as Petter Yran and John McNeece, who had both worked on the *Oriana*. All the architects working on the new project had either worked on the *Oriana* or P&O's other new ship, *Arcadia,* that had recently been transferred from the sister company Princess Cruises. The *Arcadia* gave the team plenty of experience in creating the required ambience on board. SMC were to be responsible for many of the new ship's public rooms, including coming up with something extra special for the atrium. Petter Yran took responsibility for the cabins, both formal restaurants and the nightclub whilst John

McNeece was again charged with Anderson's Bar and bringing the 'Britishness' to the overall design.

It was immediately decided that the new ship should be larger than the *Oriana* with more cabins and extra passenger facilities. The new design incorporated the same number of decks as the earlier vessel but with a few minor changes to the public rooms. Lord Sterling chose the name *Aurora* as she was to be the first ship of the new millennium and the Roman Goddess of the Dawn seemed to be the perfect choice. The new ship would be ten metres longer bringing her length up to 270 metres and her gross tonnage up to 76,512. The *Oriana* had 912 cabins, 118 of them with their own private balcony. Despite the additional cost of having a balcony, it was clear that passengers were prepared to pay the extra for this little bit of private luxury and on every *Oriana* cruise these were amongst the first grades of cabin to be sold out so the number of cabins with this feature on the new ship was to be dramatically enlarged to 406. This meant that above Deck 9 the width of the hull would have to be increased from 32.2 metres to 33.6 metres to accommodate the extra space required for all the additional balconies. Tea and coffee facilities would also be available in all grades of cabin and 24-hour dining was also to be introduced with a new bistro as a dining alternative to the main restaurants. Dining alfresco was also brought to the new ship with a Pennant Grill designed into the outer deck space looking over the ship's stern. Lighting specialists were employed to improve the internal lighting and it was they who put forward the innovative idea of 'mood' lighting where computers controlled the amount of light within the ship depending on what time of day it was and where the ship was positioned on the globe.

A new level of luxury was to be added with two new multi-level penthouses at the forward end of the ship. These were to have private balconies on two decks, a bar area, luxury living area and a dining area for up to six people. With each suite offering around 900 square feet of space they really were to be the last word in luxury and something that would make cruising with P&O more appealing to the more affluent passengers who really did demand the very best in opulence when travelling. To distinguish each cabin from the other, one would have a baby grand piano installed whilst the second would have its own personal music library to be played on a state-of-the-art music system.

With the *Oriana* starting her cruises in Britain, it was often two days into a cruise before passengers could use the open-air swimming pools due to the predominantly cold weather around the British Isles. It was therefore decided that the *Aurora* would have a retractable roof over her main swimming pool so that this popular feature could be used in any weather as soon as the ship left Southampton. Also, the Crow's Nest Lounge was moved

*The **Aurora**'s portside giant spade rudder sits under the hull immediately behind the propeller. They are electronically controlled from the navigational bridge and work simultaneously with the ship's thrusters to control all movement of the ship. (Meyer Werft)*

54

directly over the navigation bridge in place of the spa which was moved closer to the swimming pools, meaning that passengers received an improved and uninterrupted view out over the ship's bow.

AN ADVANCED SHIP FOR A NEW CENTURY

On the engineering side the ship was completely redesigned. This time diesel electric was chosen as the preferred choice of propulsion rather than engines and gearboxes, although the *Aurora* would still have shafts and rudders rather than Azipod propulsion. Out went the father and son engine arrangement in favour of four V14 M.A.N heavy marine diesel engines. Each weighs 209 tonnes and produces 14,700kW of power giving the ship a total output of 58,800kW or 79,860hp. All this power is turned into electricity, some of which is used for propulsion, the rest to power the hotel and services. The propulsion is through two A.E.G 20,000kW electric motors which in turn power the shafts to the propellers, leaving over 18,800kW of power for the passenger side. Unlike the *Oriana*, the *Aurora*'s propellers are five bladed instead of four but are fixed pitch as the electric motors control the speed and direction of the shaft. For the first time on a P&O ship, the bridge wings that extend from either side of the ship and allow the officers to see the length of the vessel, were to be enclosed. The principal reason for this was the amount of sensitive and sophisticated electronic equipment that was required on the *Aurora*'s navigation bridge. Of course, it also meant that the crew remained dry and warm in all weathers which no doubt met with great approval.

Since the *Oriana* had entered service the environmental regulations had been tightened for all passenger ships so the waste and recycling plant on the *Aurora* was upgraded to meet the new rules. Aboard the *Aurora*, all burnable waste was to be incinerated. The ship's incinerators were a step forward from other ships by the fact that they could burn different materials at the same time. Food waste was also burnt and slow feed mechanisms ensured that the smoke emissions were kept

Previous pages:

*Page 52: Taken from under the hull of the **Aurora**, a unique ship builder's view of the ship's bow is seen from the floor of the building dock. (Meyer Werft)*

Page 53: In early January 2000 the first new cruise ship of the new Millennium starts her out docking from Meyer Werft's indoor building hall. Note her funnel waiting to be lowered onto the superstructure outside the dock entrance. (Meyer Werft)

*This page: The sheer size of Meyer Werft's building dock can be appreciated in this photo as it entirely covers the new **Aurora**. Ships of up to 100,000 tonnes can be built in here. The new building hall built in 2001 can accommodate ships of over 150,000 tonnes. (Meyer Werft)*

*The **Aurora** was undocked on 6th January 2000. Her more profiled stern was one of the changes made to the outline of the ship by the Swedish designer Anders Johansson. (Meyer Werft)*

to a minimum. To control the soot emissions from the funnel, the *Aurora* was to be fitted with a revolutionary infrasonic system that set up a low frequency every five minutes. This minimises the amount of soot released into the atmosphere.

Early drawings of the *Aurora* showed the spa area above the bridge with the Crow's Nest Bar as with the *Oriana*. However, it was Anders Johansson who decided to move this area down to one of the pool areas to give the ship a smoother outline. He also redesigned the forward end of the *Aurora* to be more aerodynamic. Other external changes included rounding off the top of her funnel to line up neatly with the raking stern decks while the forward balconies and windows were also profiled to give the ship an exciting and streamlined appearance. Once the basic design of the ship had been approved, the drawings were sent out to several European yards for tender. As Meyer Werft had built the *Oriana*, they always had an advantage over the other shipyards and in April 1997 it was formally announced that the yard had won the contract to build the new ship.

A NEW SHIP FOR THE MILLENNIUM

The steel cutting for the *Aurora* began in the summer of 1998 some two years before the contractual date to finish the ship. She was to be built in the same construction hall as her sister and like the *Oriana* she was

to be built by the modular block principle with a total of 60 blocks to be used in the construction. The first block was officially laid on 15th December 1998 in front of 130 invited guests who were no doubt extremely grateful for the huge indoor construction hall as outside the temperature had dropped to well below zero. As it was a festive time of the year, a local school orchestra played Christmas carols as Gwyn Hughes, by now the new Managing Director of P&O's cruise branch, placed a newly

*Just a few days before her River Ems passage, the **Aurora** is seen at the outfitters quay of her builders. (Meyer Werft)*

*The **Aurora** at her German builders of Meyer Werft. (Meyer Werft)*

minted sterling silver pound coin under the 400-tonne block while Bernard Meyer also placed a German mark. To continue the celebrations, the guests enjoyed a traditional German festive spread of Tafelspitzboullion, roast goose and Christollen cake. During the meal, Gwyn Hughes spoke a few words in German and presented Bernard Meyer with an engraved cut glass and silver bowl as a token of P&O's appreciation of Meyer Werft's hospitality while all guests received a silver-plated paperknife, engraved with the keel-laying details.

Thanks to improvements and efficiencies at the Meyer Werft yard, the *Aurora* was to be built in a significantly shorter time than the *Oriana*. In comparison it was 22 months between the keel laying of the *Oriana* and her undocking while with the *Aurora* the time was reduced to just 13 months, a significant improvement indeed and an indication of how fast ship building was changing. The principle was still the same though with the forward end of the ship being completed first before the engineering decks then the passenger accommodation. Once the hull was finished the cabins were installed and the ship was floated up for the first time towards the end of the summer of 1999.

With the pound now less favourable against the German mark, fewer British companies were able to tender successfully for work on the new ship and many of the contracts eventually went to local German companies.

This did not stop famous British concerns such as Brintons, Ravenhead and Wedgewood all again supplying goods and materials for the new ship and despite the construction having a more German feel about it, the end product was an entirely British affair. On 6th January 2000, only a few days into the new millennium, the *Aurora* was ready for her undocking. Like her sister the superstructure was too large to allow for the funnel to be added whilst she was in the building hall.

ANOTHER RIVER EMS 'CONVEYANCE'

By coincidence, the *Aurora* started her River Ems passage almost on exactly the same date as the *Oriana* and, just as before, over 100,000 people came to witness the spectacle as the largest ship ever built in Germany made her way down the river to Leer where, just like her sister, she would be forced to wait overnight for the next high tide. Once clear of the German mainland, she made her way to the Dutch town of Emershaven to be prepared for her sea trials. The solution to the *Oriana*'s cavitational problems had already been designed into the *Aurora* before she left Meyer Werft so that there was no chance that the excessive vibration found during her sea trials were going to surprise the engineers on this occasion.

Nevertheless, the new ship was subjected to a far more rigorous set of tests than her sister when she sailed into the North Sea in late March. Despite this, it was found

*The **Aurora** outside her builders on a cold February night in 2000. Her sea trials would take place a few days later. (Meyer Werft)*

that thanks to her modern propulsion system she was vibration free and passed all of her trials with flying colours. Eventually the *Aurora* was completed and on Saturday 15th April 2000, the handover ceremony was conducted on the open deck at the ship's stern where Bernard Meyer presented her to Gwyn Hughes in front of her 850 crew. During the ceremony several of the Pakistani crew wore their traditional dress and proudly took part in the raising of the Red Ensign before the ship finally left Holland and made her way to her new home port of Southampton.

AURORA MEETS THE TALL SHIPS

The *Aurora*'s entrance into the Solent on Sunday 16th April was as impressive as it was spectacular. She arrived off the Nab Tower early in the morning to embark her pilot before continuing along the Solent to Cowes on the Isle of Wight where she anchored alongside HMS *Glasgow*. Southampton was alive with the flotilla of the Tall Ships' Race which was to leave the port at midday, passing the *Aurora* en route for Plymouth and the start of the race across the Atlantic Ocean. Thousands of people had come out in the sunshine to watch these splendid vessels leave Southampton and sail past P&O's new 'super liner' as the *Aurora* was now being marketed. Once the last of the grand old sailing ships had passed by P&O's grand new ship, two tugs made their way out to the *Aurora* to escort her up Southampton Water and into her new home. Four water cannons sprayed continuously as the majestic new ship, the largest to be based in Southampton since Cunard's famous 'Queens' of the 1930s slowly made her way to the Queen Elizabeth II terminal which was to be

her base for the next two weeks. The crowds had actually grown since the Tall Ships had left as everyone wanted to be amongst the first to catch a glimpse of the new ship and it was with great fanfare and aplomb that she finally docked in the early afternoon.

The inaugural events committee had again been very busy and over the next week thousands of invited guests from the media and travel trade were allowed to explore the ship at their leisure. Various celebration lunches and dinners took part in which the *Aurora* was the star of the show. Her official naming ceremony was to be conducted by the Princess Royal, Princess Anne on 27th April. The night before she arrived with her husband, Commander Tim Lawrence, where she was guest of honour at a glittering gala reception hosted by Lord Sterling. The Royal party spent the night on board in one of the *Aurora*'s stunning Penthouse Suites. The following day the awful weather that had been hanging over Southampton for some time cleared away and was replaced by brilliant sunshine.

PRINCESS ANNE NAMES THE AURORA

Before the ceremony started, Princess Anne had enjoyed a behind the scenes tour of the ship and signed a photograph of herself which was placed in the Officers' Wardroom while a copy of the photo was placed in the main atrium. Just before 11.00, the Royal party was escorted to the special naming platform which had been erected on the quayside, under *Aurora*'s starboard bow while the band of Her Majesty's Royal Marines entertained the assembled guests.

The Regimental Band of the Scots Guards also played various traditional Scottish anthems whilst the Pipes and Drums of the 1st Battalion Scots Guards played El Alamein and other military numbers. The choir of Salisbury Cathedral School sang the 'Easter Hymn' with soloist Fabienne Aurora Bourget followed by the Aurora procession. This included Sir Stirling Moss being pulled in a traditional Madeira basket and a procession of 14 children, one from each country of the world visited by P&O's ships each wearing their national costumes. The P&O coat of arms was represented by a lion on a tabard, a bronze kangaroo, a ten-man Chinese dragon and an elephant. Aurora, the Roman Goddess of the Dawn then arrived in a chariot pulled by winged horses. The whole procession was thoroughly enjoyed by the distinguished guests and dignitaries who were present. The Right Reverend Dr Alan Smithson, the Bishop of Jarrow, then lead the congregation in prayer before he blessed the ship. Then Lord Sterling invited the Princess Royal forward to name the ship. Just like her mother five years previously she uttered those well-known words, "I name this ship *Aurora*. May God bless her and all who sail in her." A bottle of champagne was released against the 'R' in *Aurora* and brightly coloured

*The **Aurora** at the start of her River Ems passage to the North Sea. Just like the **Oriana** thousands of people turned out to see the giant ship leave the shipyard. (Meyer Werft)*

streamers and confetti exploded over everyone. What no one had noticed was that the champagne bottle had refused to break on the ship's hull and had quietly dropped into the water. After all the guests had gone on board for a celebratory luncheon, which was held in all three of the ship's restaurants, gifts were exchanged in the atrium where both Bernard Meyer and Lord Sterling made presentations to Princess Anne and the ship's Master, Captain Stephen Burgoine, who was presented with a traditional P&O sword to mark the auspicious occasion.

Once the festivities were completed, the *Aurora* departed on a series of short cruises to show the ship off to the media and travel trade.

TWO MAIDEN VOYAGES

Finally the day had arrived where the *Aurora* had to start earning her keep and was to set sail on her 14-night Maiden Voyage to the Mediterranean. On Monday 1st May 2000, 1,850 passengers boarded the ship ready to indulge themselves in the wonder of P&O's latest vessel. The Essex

*On 15th April 2000, Bernard Meyer hands over the owner's manual to Gwyn Hughes and the **Aurora** is officially a P&O ship. (Meyer Werft)*

*As part of the handover ceremony the German flag was lowered from the **Aurora**'s stern and replaced with the Red Ensign. (Meyer Werft)*

*The **Aurora** dressed overall as she waits in the Solent before arriving in Southampton for the first time in April 2000. (Ambrose Greenway)*

Caledonian Pipe Band played the ship away and at exactly 18.00, the ship cast her morning ropes and sounded her horn. Confetti was blasted over the ship and a glass of champagne handed to every passenger. Streamers were flung from the passenger decks and the port's tugs made sure that the departure was a spectacularly wet occasion. The *Aurora* made her way slowly down Southampton Water followed by hundreds of well wishers in small boats before turning into the Solent and the English Channel.

Unfortunately, during the early hours of Tuesday morning, just as the ship was passing the Ile d'Ouessant off the north-west coast of France and about to head into the Bay of Biscay, her engineers noticed that one of her white metal bearings in her port stern tube was overheating. If this was not corrected then it could have caused irrevocable damage to the propeller shaft but the problem could not be solved whilst the ship was at sea. The very bold, but correct, decision was therefore made to bring the ship home and have the bearing replaced immediately. On Wednesday morning the *Aurora* sailed back into Southampton and disembarked her passengers. P&O promised all of them both a full refund and a free cruise of their choice whenever they wanted to take it. Everyone was naturally disappointed but extremely pleased with the way P&O had dealt with the situation. The *Aurora* sailed for the German Shipyard of Blohm & Voss in Hamburg where she was dry-docked and the damaged bearing replaced.

She was back in Southampton in plenty of time for her next cruise on 15th May which went off without a hitch and was a great success. The *Aurora* went on to enjoy a very successful maiden season during which thousands of people enjoyed the holiday of a lifetime on her as the ship began to establish herself as a very welcome addition to the P&O fleet.

She quickly settled down to a regular sailing pattern of Mediterranean cruises with the mid-summer trips to the Norwegian fjords and autumnal sailings to New England in America as well as the traditional world cruise in January. Even today, thanks to her unique design and solid construction, she is one of the most graceful-looking ships seen sailing out of Southampton and one of the few vessels that actually look like an ocean-going passenger ship. Her exceptionally well-designed hull means that even in the worst of a Bay of Biscay storm the *Aurora* has been

*Left: The **Aurora** makes a splendid sight as she sails through the English Channel and out into the Atlantic Ocean on another Mediterranean cruise from Southampton. (FotoFlite)*

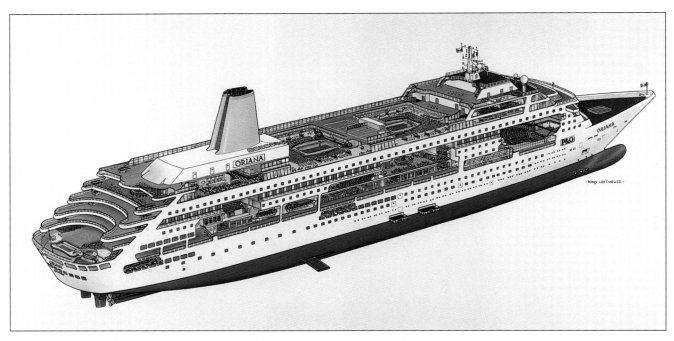

*A cutaway drawing of the **Oriana** showing some of her larger public rooms. (Meyer Werft)*

noted to be rather more steady than any of the other cruise ships currently sailing out of the UK. Put simply, she has sea-keeping qualities that are second to none.

UNIQUE SHIPS

Today the *Oriana* and the *Aurora* are approaching the mid-life points in their careers with P&O Cruises. They are no longer registered in London but in the Bermudan city of Hamilton to allow weddings at sea to take place which

have become very popular over the last decade or so. The *Oriana* has just been refitted with over £25 million being spent on her to upgrade her to modern cruise standards and to adapt her for her new roll as an exclusively for adults ship. The *Aurora* will soon require a similar amount of money being spent on her to allow her to enter the second half of her career and still keep her up to date with the latest cruise and lifestyle trends. As P&O Cruises is now part of the Carnival brand of companies it is a

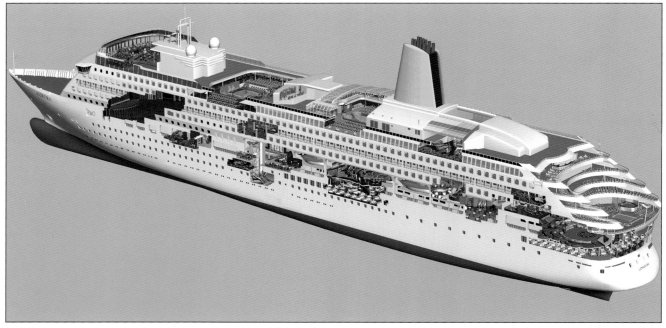

*A cutaway drawing of the **Aurora** with her large retractable glass roof over the swimming pool clearly visible. (Meyer Werft)*

*The **Aurora** has to go for a major overhaul every five years. She is seen at the German Shipyard of Lloyd Werft having just completed her overhall of 2005. (Lloyd Werft)*

realistic fact that ships like these will never be built again as all new builds will be from a universal design which can be used throughout the company's other brands such as Cunard, Holland America Line or Princess Cruises. Indeed since Carnival Corporation took over, all new ships that have entered service for P&O Cruises have come from a design which has been used by one of these companies. To build a one-off ship to a unique design such as the *Oriana* or the *Aurora* is simply too expensive. The *Oriana* was the

first cruise ship designed and built exclusively for the British market and the *Aurora* was a development of this extremely successful ship. They are without doubt truly British cruise ships which are loved by their passengers and their crews respectively. They were built in a time when it was important that a ship looked like a ship and their graceful and beautiful lines were as important as the facilities offered to their passengers. We will never see anything quite like them again.

*Situated in the innermost part of Norway's Aurlandsfjord we see the **Aurora** at the tranquil town of Flam. (P&O Cruises)*

Aurora & Oriana

Interior Design for the British Passengers

No matter how beautiful a ship is on the outside, it is her interiors that passengers really enjoy and appreciate. The co-ordinating interior architect for both the *Oriana* and the *Aurora* was the Swedish architect, the late Robert Tillberg. He was very much hands on with the design of the *Oriana* but for the *Aurora* he allowed Anders Johansson to take most of the design leads.

Robert Tillberg was himself a true pioneering spirit and inventor who challenged both owners and shipyards to make sure that his clients achieved the best possible product for the money they invested. He became involved early on in the process so that things were completed to his very high standards right from the very beginning. Tillberg had designed the very first atrium on a passenger ship back in 1969 when he was the lead architect on the *Sea Venture*. It was only two decks high but when he presented the idea to the engineers at the shipyard, they laughed and told him it was impossible to build a ship with such a big hole in the middle. Robert quietly asked them, "Do you not also build oil tankers? Do they not also have a big hole in the middle?" He developed numerous systems such as modular wall panels, ceiling systems and a multitude of decorative finishes that make it possible to achieve elegant interiors that are also practical and durable. Most are still used today and examples of his work can be seen on many of the world's cruise ships.

Tillberg was the natural choice for P&O to design the passenger spaces for the *Oriana* and the *Aurora*. He decided to bring in British architect John McNeece to help with the design of some of the public rooms and to stamp an overall feeling of Britishness to the whole theme whilst the Norwegian architect Petter Yran was asked to design the cabins on both ships as well as the restaurants and other selected public rooms on the *Aurora*.

When British passengers go on board a ship they expect it to look like a ship and not like a floating hotel, so with this in mind the three architects adopted a more ship-like design in their drawings. In the cabins there were no sharp corners on the furniture and there were arches which were reminiscent of traditional sailing ships. Modern laminates that looked like wood were extensively used and both the *Oriana* and the *Aurora* were to have more baths in their cabins than any other cruise ship because the British prefer to have baths whilst most foreign passengers prefer showers. Classic textile patterns have been used throughout the ships along with strong colours, but none of the public rooms have polished metals, neon lights or any of the glitzy razzmatazz that you find on American-based cruise ships. Both ships are one class but in an effort to please everyone, certain areas have been designed to appeal more to some passengers then to others. For example, the Anderson's Bar has been designed to look and feel like a traditional London gentlemen's club whilst the sports bar has a fast, modern cosmopolitan feel with a completely different atmosphere.

*The Thackeray Room on the **Oriana** is named after the Victorian writer William Makepeace Thackeray, whose writing gave the company a lot of much needed publicity. The furniture was designed by the Queen's nephew, Lord Lindley. (Brian D. Smith)*

*Top left: The Tiffany Bar sits at the top of the **Oriana**'s main atrium and is so named as its ceiling is made from beautiful Tiffany-style glass. (Brian D. Smith)*

*Top right: On the **Oriana**, delicate crystal glass is used in the Curzon Room where passengers can enjoy the very finest of foods created by Marco Pierre White. (Brian D. Smith)*

*Above: The two main restaurants on the **Oriana** are named Peninsular and Oriental. (Brian D. Smith)*

*Right: Outside the Lord's Tavern on the **Oriana** is a cricket hall of fame with paintings of Ian Botham, Graham Gooch and Brian Lara. (Brian D. Smith)*

BRITISH SHIPS – BRITISH MARKET

At the time of the *Oriana*'s construction almost all new cruise ships were being designed for the North American market whose trend was to go for much larger rooms where large numbers of passengers could mix at the same time. This is why P&O Cruises' ships have several main restaurants whilst American ships normally have one vast restaurant over several decks.

American ships also have much larger casinos, theatres and bars but a much smaller amount of outside deck space as they like to enjoy inside pursuits whilst the British public prefer to sunbathe more than anything else when they are on holiday. Consequently, British ships have a larger amount of outside deck space for the passengers to enjoy their favourite pastimes.

Robert Tillberg stated at the time of the *Oriana*'s inauguration that when designing the ship's interiors he had wanted to create an entrance and an atrium that customers would never forget. He said, "I think it is very important that the first impression that a passenger gets when they enter a ship is the size, the quality and the openness of the ship." So at the heart of the *Oriana* he

*Left: Sorrento's is a new alternative dining venue created on the **Oriana** during her mid-life refit of 2011.(Brian D. Smith)*

*Above: Robert Tillberg's four-deck high atrium at the heart of the **Oriana** creates a highly sophisticated ambience for her passengers to enjoy. (Brian D. Smith)*

designed the ship's impressive four-storey atrium, with its magnificent waterfall, lush subtropical plantings and Tiffany-styled glass. It is truly imposing and sets the feel for the lavishness of the ship. A striking curved staircase weaves its way up though the passenger decks which as you walk down, truly takes your breath away. The use of light marble and real wood combines with discrete lighting to create the perfect ambience for your holiday. The ship's reception desk is situated adjacent to the atrium as well as the Tiffany Court where passengers can take morning coffee, afternoon tea or something stronger. In addition, there is

the shopping centre known as Knightsbridge which gives the atrium a sense of purpose as well as being the heart of the ship's passenger area.

The atrium on the *Aurora* is also truly stunning. It too rises over four decks and is decorated in warm shades of gold, bronze and pale coffee that strengthen as you go upwards. The centrepiece is a 12-metre Lalique-style sculpture of two mythical figures behind a veil of water. The cream marble grand staircase sweeps down in front of the sculpture giving passengers the chance to marvel at this wonderful spectacle close up. Polished Crema Marfil marble

columns rise up to Deck 8 which opens out to the Raffles coffee and chocolate bar. It is the perfect place to look down on the wonder of human life that passes through the centre of the ship each day. Also featured in the *Aurora*'s atrium is Charlie's Champagne Bar where a decorative glass balustrade welcomes you whilst a marble and granite floor borders leather-covered chairs and a baby grand piano is played every night before dinner. Both atriums, although very different, give passengers a taste of the style and opulence they can expect whilst on board and certainly create that 'wow' feeling which is so sadly missing from a lot of cruise ships today.

PUBS, CLUBS AND GAMES

Moving away from the atriums on both ships you soon come across other particularly quaint essentially British touches which make the *Oriana* and *Aurora* so distinctive. The Lord's Tavern on the *Oriana* was a development of the Cricketer's Pub on board the former P&O vessel, the *Canberra*, and was designed by John McNeece to have an idiosyncratically British feel. This is accentuated by the fact that there are five large windows onto the veranda where there are tables and chairs to sit at with large white cricket umbrellas. Artist Janet Shearer visited Lord's cricket ground to watch several matches before painting her large mural, depicting the view from the upper stand looking towards the scoreboard and the clubhouse. The striped green carpet certainly resembles a cricket field and even the handrails around the bar have a cricket ball at their ends. One of the pub's main features is an awning above the bar which is a replica of the famous Mound Stand adding to the overall effect of the bar and leaving you in no doubt as to what cricket ground your drinking establishment really should be in.

This area was so popular that it was extended during the refit of 2006 to encompass the Jackpot Casino room which was moved to another location on the ship. Outside the Lord's Tavern is a cricket hall of fame with paintings of three of the world's most famous cricketers: Ian Botham, Graham Gooch and Brian Lara.

On the *Aurora* it was decided to go for the popular sports bar which you can now find in most British city centres. Named Champions, it has multiple television screens around the room showing live sporting action from across the globe. Wooden bar stools surround the curved bar with tables and chairs spread across a wavy blue carpet designed to give a nautical theme. This area is very popular when any major sporting event is taking place such as Wimbledon, the Olympic Games or the Football World Cup. Although not totally dedicated to cricket there

*Left: Artist Janet Shearer visited Lord's cricket ground to watch several matches before painting her large mural of the ground as the **Oriana**'s Lord's Tavern defining feature. (Brian D. Smith)*

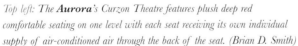

*Top left: The **Aurora**'s Curzon Theatre features plush deep red comfortable seating on one level with each seat receiving its own individual supply of air-conditioned air through the back of the seat. (Brian D. Smith)*

*Top right: Both the **Oriana** and the **Aurora** have cinemas showing the most popular films from the big screen. Here we see the entrance to **Aurora**'s Playhouse Cinema. (Miles Cowsill)*

*Above: The **Aurora**'s Crystal Pool has a retractable glass roof meaning that the pool can be used at any time, day or night in all weathers. (Brian D. Smith)*

*Right: The Pennant bar situated at the top of **Aurora**'s stern is the perfect place to enjoy P&O's famous sail away parties. (Brian D. Smith)*

is other sports memorabilia on display from golf to motor racing making this venue extremely fashionable with some of Aurora's younger guests.

Another popular venue is the Crow's Nest Bar which is situated high up above the navigational bridge on each ship at around 32 metres above the waterline. The glass wall which sweeps round 270 degrees of the bar gives the most outstanding views to sea for around 300 people with seating on two levels so that as many people as possible can enjoy the panoramic spectacular without having to fight for a front seat view. Each room is decorated with

nautical memorabilia celebrating P&O Cruises' history such as the illuminated model of the *Ranpura* which sits behind the bar on the *Oriana* whilst on the *Aurora* there is a model of the *Strathnaver*, the first of five sister ships ordered by P&O in the 1930s. A genuine ship's binnacle sits in front of the bar whilst a domed ceiling in the centre of the room depicts the night sky which changes depending on what hemisphere you are in. Dark cherry wood combines with rich soft fabrics to create a luxurious but relaxed atmosphere which during the day is a quiet and informal place, perfect for an early coffee or for

*Above left: Bright colourful artwork is used throughout the **Aurora**'s Orangery to create a very vibrant atmosphere in the self-service restaurant. (Brian D. Smith)*

*Above: On the **Aurora**, Petter Yran took a Moorish theme as the inspiration for the Medina Restaurant with deep Moroccan curtains hanging from the dividers and the windows. (Brian D. Smith)*

relaxing whilst you take in the ever-changing view of the sea. During the evening, it livens up completely with pre-dinner drinks parties on gala nights and live music for the less formal occasions which can go on well into the early hours.

The deep richness of Anderson's Bar can be found on the Promenade Deck and is one of John McNeece's masterpieces. It is named after Arthur Anderson, a founder member of the Peninsular and Oriental Steam Navigation Company who would no doubt appreciate both the portrait and a specially commissioned bust of himself as

well as the series of 19th-century marine paintings of P&O ships which hang on the wall of the club. The decor is designed to create the atmosphere of a discrete and intimate Victorian gentlemen's club that you would have found in London at around the turn of the 20th century. There are plenty of traditionally designed armchairs upholstered in Regency patterns and flanked by period-style tables fashioned in mahogany. A lighter oak is used for the panelling and bar area whilst on the *Aurora* there is even a white marble fireplace, a feature found on very few large passenger ships.

RESTAURANTS OF CHOICE

One of the great delights of cruising with P&O Cruises is enjoying the high-quality cuisine which the company offers on all of its ships. Creating a great dining establishment is no simple task as you need to create a serene setting, elegantly designed to welcome diners with an ambience of taste and comfort.

On the *Oriana*, the restaurants were designed by Robert Tillberg and named the Peninsular and the Oriental whilst on the *Aurora*, Petter Yran was given the opportunity to show his flair in the Medina and the Alexandria. Both ships' main restaurants are situated on the same deck with the galley located in between the two so that each is served equally with tables for two, four, six, eight or ten people so that passenger seating requests can be accommodated whenever possible. Each has its own particular feel and own way of seducing you towards the main event of any day as congenial surroundings can be as important as the food to make a memorable occasion. The Peninsular Restaurant has as its centrepiece a classic landscape painting of The Journey of Odysseus by Rose Warnock which stretches the whole length of the wall facing the entrance to the restaurant and which dominates the room. An individual light on each table works well with the large crystal chandelier which hangs in the centre of the room giving just the right amount of light to create a very intimate but well-lit atmosphere. The main feature of the Oriental Restaurant is the large open windows on three sides giving passengers wonderful unobstructed views of the sea. On the *Aurora*, Petter Yran took a Moorish theme as the inspiration for the Medina Restaurant with a double entrance stairway sweeping down from the portside of the ship against a stunning backdrop of vibrantly coloured stained glass. This design is taken up on the pillars between the windows and the glass panelled dividers that help to create more of a cosy feeling. Over in the Alexandria Restaurant inspiration has been taken from the world of the pharaohs with lotus blossom images and shaped planters along with a jewel rich carpet which works well with the soft gold of the upholstery. Just like the *Oriana*'s Oriental Restaurant, there are large widows on three sides giving you unrivalled views to sea.

Up on the *Aurora*'s Lido Deck the ship's buffet restaurant called the Orangery covers the full width of the ship with the serving area based around a series of serving islands set diagonally across the floor to ensure that the maximum amount of people can be served at one time. The carpet, chairs and tables are all very brightly coloured and create a very different mood to the rest of the ship. The innovative use of a dance floor in the dining area means that during the evening this area turns into an alternative dining area where entertainment is provided. A sidewalk café is situated next to the Orangery on the starboard side of the ship serving top quality fast food which can be very handy during the day. On the *Oriana* there is the Conservatory which, like the Orangery on the *Aurora*, is the ship's main buffet area and is situated between the Crystal Pool and the Terrance Bar. With a combination of vibrant modern murals depicting the English countryside painted by the British artist Colin Failes and full-length glass walls, it too changes to an informal self-service restaurant in the evening offering another alternative dining venue.

During her recent refit at Hamburg, the rear of the port side of the conservatory was turned into a waiter service restaurant called Sorrento's. By day this area is open to customers using the buffet but in the evening it becomes an area of select dining where passengers can choose to enjoy fine Italian food for a small extra charge.

Both ships have restaurants by the celebrity chef Marco Pierre White. On the *Oriana* it was the former Curzon Room which was transformed into this signature restaurant during her conversion to an exclusively for adults ship and features a series of Indian embroideries by Alice Kettle along with a selection of elephant statues which go a long way to celebrate the company's Indian heritage. On the *Aurora*, the former Café Bordeaux, which was the first 24-hour café at sea ever to be offered to the British public, oozes the charm of a traditional Paris bistro whilst serving Marco's unique take on superior British dining; this is where Gallic flair meets exceptional British cuisine. Entrance is via a sweeping circular staircase handsomely panelled in chequered squares of polished wood from the deck below or the smart, elegant walkway that doubles as the photo gallery. Both venues offer smaller, more intimate places where people can look forward to something very different when choosing where to dine.

An alternative to dining inside is to enjoy the Terraced Bar Grill in the evening. By day they are popular destinations in their own right as each is situated on the Lido Deck overlooking the raked stern and swimming pool giving great views out over the ship's wake. With wooden teak floors and leather bar stools, terrace tables and waiter service it can be very difficult to find a seat on a sea day or at lunchtime as the natural design of the ship makes them very sheltered spots to enjoy the outside life. By night they are both turned into luxurious restaurants where the very best in fresh food is served.

WEST END STYLE ENTERTAINMENT

All modern cruise ships have a theatre and the *Oriana* and the *Aurora* are no exception. As Robert Tillberg had

*Right: The **Aurora**'s atrium is truly stunning, rising through four decks and featuring a 12-metre high Lalique-style sculpture of two mythical figures behind a veil of water. (Brian D. Smith)*

*The **Oriana**'s atrium features a beautiful Tiffany-style glass ceiling, a waterfall and tropical plants. The gold seahorses are part of the ship's Christmas decorations for 2011. (Brian D. Smith)*

very little experience in stage design, he brought in theatre designer John Wyckham to advise on the seating layout, acoustics and lighting for the Royal and Curzon Theatres. One of the first things he did was to remove two of the four supporting columns from the original design on the *Oriana* to improve sightlines. The theatres each seat 650 people on one level in plush deep red seats with each seat receiving its own individual supply of air conditioned air through the back of the seat. There are no drinks holders or bar in either theatre because the head of P&O's entertainment did not want anything to detract from the top quality entertainment the company provided for its passengers. The stage on both

A genuine White marble fireplace us the main feature of the Aurora's Anderson's Bar. (Brian D Smith)

ships is 24 metres wide and on the *Aurora* there is a fly loft to move the scenery. The rich colour schemes and fabric designs draw heavily on the traditions of the British theatre, both of which were chosen for their dramatic effect. One interesting note is that the area under the raked theatre floor is used to store over 1,000 costumes.

KEEPING FIT

One of the big advances in cruise ship design over the last 20 years or so has been the development of the Well Being or Spa area. Previously, this area might have been a small gym offering the basic keep fit equipment with a diminutive indoor pool, normally reserved for those passengers travelling First Class. Today it is a vast area with huge gyms and every conceivable piece of cardiovascular fitness machine for people of all ages. There are saunas, hydrotherapy pools, thermal relaxation suites, hairdressers and every other imaginable feature designed to enhance you time on board. Aboard the *Oriana* this facility is situated at the extreme forward end of the Lido Deck and was originally run by the famous health club, Champneys. Today it is under the control of P&O Cruises and divided into three distinct areas; the hair salon, the beauty and massage rooms and the relaxation area containing the gymnasium and aerobics rooms. All were originally decked out in the art deco theme of the 1930s with much use of stainless steel, glass and light fittings from the period.

At the front of the spa is a relaxation area with two Jacuzzi pools and cane furniture looking over the front of

the ship. In the centre of this area there used to be a curved chrome balustrade, the glass panels of which featured an art deco motif formed around a circular fountain with a figure of a woman. This was all removed during the spa's refit of December 2011 and is now a modern seating area with comfortable full-length relaxation beds in black and green. Behind the old fountain area is the entrance to the sauna and hydrotherapy area where five private therapy rooms offer a range of specialist treatments.

On the *Aurora*, the Oasis Spa and Weights and Measures Gym were moved to the centre of the ship and are situated over two decks overlooking the Riviera Pool. With the look of a botanical garden, green plants are now tastefully displayed around the entrance and exercise stations with the gymnasium and aerobics room on the lower level giving access directly to the pool. This fantastic idea allows customers to work out in the gym, shower before going for a swim in the open air pool then finish off their fitness experience with a drink from the Riviera Bar which is situated right next to the pool. Above the aerobics area is a curved marble staircase leading up to the hair and beauty section and the private therapy rooms where the same treatments are offered as on the *Oriana*. Fitness instructors are on duty at all times on both ships to offer advice and run the daily programmes that are devised for each particular cruise.

OTHER ENTERTAINMENT AREAS

Another popular pastime whilst on a cruise is to enjoy the fun and excitement of a real casino. Both ships have these vibrant areas which on the *Aurora* is situated next to Champions Sports Bar whilst on the *Oriana* it was originally next to the Lord's Tavern in a similar position but when this room was increased in size in 2006, it was moved to the Monte Carlo Room next to Anderson's Bar. With over 70 slot machines and tables for roulette and various card games, they are distinctly smaller than the average casino found on most American cruise ships. The British tend to prefer more traditional enjoyments such as bridge or solitaire.

To cater for the popular British pastimes, games rooms

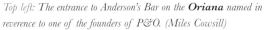

Top left: The entrance to Anderson's Bar on the **Oriana** *named in reverence to one of the founders of P&O. (Miles Cowsill)*

Above right: Anderson's Bar on the **Aurora** *was designed by John McNeece to have the feel of a London gentleman's club. (Miles Cowsill)*

Above left: The Sports bar Champions on the **Aurora** *features brightly coloured contemporary furniture and shows live sporting action from around the world. (Miles Cowsill)*

Right: The library on the **Aurora** *features a large number of books and board games as well as comfortable furniture to sit and enjoy the facilities. (Miles Cowsill)*

are situated around the ship where passengers can not only play card games but also engage in other popular pursuits such as chess and backgammon. As well as games rooms there are also libraries and quiet rooms such as the Thackeray Room on the *Oriana*, named after the Victorian writer William Makepeace Thackeray, who was one of P&O's first passengers and whose writing gave the company a lot of much needed publicity. Like the library it is furnished with furniture from David Linley where a distinctly green and gold theme with beautiful dark polished wood and a tartan carpet gives the room a stately home look and certainly relaxes you for an

afternoon's reading. There is also the card room called Crichton's named after the former P&O director Sir Andrew Crichton, where the wooden tables have chessboards built into their surfaces so that games like draughts and, of course, chess can be played. The room can be divided into two so that passengers can continue to play their favourite games whilst organised games tournaments can also take place in the other half. The *Aurora* has a card room of a similar nature called Vanderbilt's which is two separate rooms with the same colour theme as her sister.

The libraries on both ships have around 4,000 books

*Above left: During the **Oriana**'s refit of 2011 a new alternative dining venue was created in the Conservatory on Deck 11 serving fine Italian cuisine. (Brian D. Smith)*

*Left: For the evening dinner service, the **Aurora**'s Orangery offers an informal alternative dining venue for passengers looking for a more relaxed occasion. (Brian D. Smith)*

*Above: A circular fountain with a figure of a woman complements the Art Deco design of the well-being area on the **Oriana**. This was removed during the 2011 refit. (Brian D. Smith)*

meaning that there are enough for every passenger to have two books each and still leave enough for someone else to make a selection. The rooms are furnished with built-in walnut veneer bookcases especially designed for each ship with glass doors that fold away neatly when not in use. On the *Oriana* a large octagonal inlaid wood table and companion designed and built by the Queen's nephew, David Linley, sits in the centre of the room which without any windows to allow in any natural light is the room's most distinguishing feature. On the *Aurora* the library was moved to the starboard side of the ship allowing for large floor to ceiling windows to be installed

which greatly improved the ambience of the room. Tables and chairs were installed giving people the option of remaining in the library and reading there if they wished to do so.

High up on the Lido Deck are the Uganda Room on the *Aurora* and the Medina Room on the *Oriana*. They are small, intimate rooms situated next to the Crow's Nest Bars and it is in rooms like this that marriages at sea will normally take place as well as any religious services that are conducted throughout the cruise. Both have floor to ceiling windows and an abundance of natural light making them very bright and airy rooms that can be used for private functions such as birthday parties or anniversaries. The rooms have a more nautical theme than the rest of the ship with a model of the two P&O ships after which each room is named on prominent display as well as a rich use of warm woods, especially the gold trimmed bubinga wood panels which were used so predominantly in both vessels. Paintings of past P&O ships celebrating the company's history combine with a mixture of dark rich reds and blues to complete the maritime ensemble.

NIGHTCLUBS

One of many pleasures that can be enjoyed on a cruise ship is the opportunity to dance and on both the

*Fine art is all around P&O Cruises' ships and is depicted here with a statue of two dancers at the entrance to the **Aurora's** Carmen Lounge. (Miles Cowsill)*

Oriana and the *Aurora* there are several places where customers can engage in this rewarding exercise. Both ships have large show rooms seating around 450 people with generously sized dance floors situated on the Promenade Deck at the stern.

Named the Pacific Lounge on the *Oriana* and Carmen's on the *Aurora*, each have significant sound and light systems to create just the right ambience for the type of dancing that is taking place. The house band is usually set up on the raised stage area whilst the seating around the dance floor is slightly raked on three levels with high-backed bench seating and tables. There is a bar in each room with a standing area for those who don't like to sit down and enjoy their drink whilst watching the entertainment. Carmen's has more occasional furniture than high-backed seating with a mixture of glass and wooden tables in a range of vibrant colours giving a very eclectic look to the whole room whilst the Pacific Lounge was refitted in 2011 with new cream, gold and red furniture which blends in very nicely and creates a very warm and welcoming environment.

Further forward on the *Oriana* is another dance room called Harlequins which also doubles up as the ship's nightclub. This is one of John McNeece's works of genius as he has managed to design a room with a large open space with a beautiful parquet dance floor containing a star and diamond motif for such pastimes as ballroom dancing during the day but which can also be reduced in size to a much smaller and more intimate space when used as a

nightclub. There is a stage where performers can sing as well as a disc jockey booth for the nightclub usage. A multitude of warm colours work well with the artificial light in a similar fashion to the Pacific Lounge to create the desired ambience.

On the *Aurora* the space of Harlequins is replaced with an all-singing and dancing nightclub called Masquerades. The entrance is extremely ostentatious with a large blue and gold metallic mural which really sets the scene for what is inside. There are banks of bright neon lights with orange and purple furniture to create a high-energy atmosphere. The dance floor is a multitude of flashing coloured lights with a sound system that really drives the atmosphere to another level. On some of *Aurora's* longer cruises this room can be seriously under used as it is not too unfair to say that the majority of passengers no longer go to nightclubs for entertainment. However, on a short party cruise the place is usually jumping with an atmosphere that simply cannot be beaten anywhere else.

SWIMMING POOLS

One of the reasons that the *Oriana* and the *Aurora* are so popular with the British cruising public is the amount of outside deck space available for passengers to enjoy whilst on board. They both have beautiful teak promenade decks going right around the ship on Deck 7 where passengers obtain the most spectacular views close to the bow as they are only about 15 metres above the sea. You can experience the most exhilarating feeling watching the ships cutting through the water as the bow wave moves along the hull and it is also the most likely place to get a close-up of marine wildlife such as whales and dolphins. Most deep-sea passenger vessels have their open passenger decks high up on Decks 12 or above and, even when it comes close, passengers are usually too distant to observe marine wildlife. There are also a large number of deckchairs and deck beds here with deep comfortable mattresses allowing passengers to make themselves comfortable whilst watching nature's great display.

As well as the Promenade Deck there are the open

areas on Decks 12 and 13 where it is possible to find wide areas for sunbathing as well as golf nets, sports courts, swimming pools, Jacuzzis, various bars and eating establishments as well as works of art. The main swimming pool on the *Oriana* was the largest pool ever built on a passenger ship when she entered service in 1995 whilst the *Aurora* has a retractable roof over her main pool which can be closed during inclement periods meaning that this popular feature can be used during any cruise whatever the weather. Unlike most cruise ships the *Oriana* and the *Aurora* have a third swimming pool on their sterns on Deck 8 which is surrounded by a large teak deck and its own bar serving drinks for those too tired to walk up to the Terrace Bar on the Lido Deck. It is here that many people will gather for the 'Sail Away Parties' that P&O Cruises are so famous for every time a ship leaves port.

*Right: Built as one of four Jubilee ships to celebrate Queen Victoria's Golden Jubilee, P&O's first **Arcadia** is depicted here at the entrance to the **Aurora**'s Anderson's Bar. (Miles Cowsill)*

CABINS

All the passenger and crew cabins were designed by Petter Yran who was given a design brief to create cabins which emphasised timeless elegance with a British flavour but were in no way old fashioned. It meant using solid colours rather than pastels which are usually found in American ships as well as classic textures and fabrics with as much high-quality wood as possible, particularly in the suites. There are more women cruising than men which is why Petter Yran went for the feminine touch right from the start. He explained, "Women are the passengers who really care about how the ship and in particular the cabins look and function. We made sure the artwork was softer with paintings of flowers rather than buildings and made sure that there was plenty of storage and hanging space."

The *Oriana* has 730 twin bedded cabins which can easily be converted to a double, depending on the passenger's choice. Of these 132 have two beds located in the ceiling which can be used to accommodate up to four people, 66 are a slightly higher grade known as a stateroom and eight have been specially adapted for use by disabled people. A total of 476 are outside cabins with a large picture window and 320 are positioned inside the ship. All cabins have a private bathroom with toilet and

shower with a significant number also having a full-size bath. Each cabin has been designed to optimise the available floor space which is approximately 150 square feet. There is a distinct sitting area away from the beds to create the sense of space with soft furnishings including the curtains and scatter cushions colour co-ordinated in pale tones of blue and taupe to harmonise with the fixed furniture of light beach wood and occasional brass. Each bed has its own bedside cabinet and reading light which can be controlled from the main switch or remotely by the bed.

On the *Aurora* there is a similar twin bedded arrangement but with a new grade of cabin which includes a private balcony. Some 272 of these cabins are available meaning that over 40 per cent of cabins have a private balcony. As the beds on a balconied cabin have to be longitudinal rather than latitudinal, the cabins are slightly wider and have a total space of 211 square feet, including the balcony of around 40 square feet which has two patio chairs and a small table as deck furniture.

For some, a cabin is just a place to sleep and change but for others, it is a place to enjoy the ultimate in gracious living. The Britannia Deck on both ships comprises entirely of deluxe cabins and suites and was specifically chosen because it is one of the quietest areas on board.

The deluxe balcony cabin grade has larger bathrooms and a larger seating area in a wider cabin with three large French windows which lead out onto a generously proportioned balcony furnished with more luxurious deck furniture for you to enjoy. An atlas of the world and a pair of binoculars are also available. There are 94 of these cabins on the *Oriana* whilst the *Aurora* has two more. In the mini suite, customers can enjoy up to 368 square feet of space as well as a whirlpool bath and ironing facilities. Beautifully decorated in soothing shades of either apricot and gold or crimson and blue, there is also a coffee machine and a DVD player for extra enjoyment. Wonderful wooden arches that cross the entire cabin divide the bedroom from the living area as well as the full-width glass wall that leads out onto the balcony. The *Oriana* has 16 of these suites to offer whilst the *Aurora* has 20.

*Top right: The graceful raked stern on the **Oriana** is the perfect place to watch the ships wake as you sail from one destination to another. (William Mayes)*

Above: The promenade Deck on Deck 7 is a very popular place on both ships to enjoy the sea air in relative shelter. (P&O Cruises)

*Right: The **Aurora**'s two Penthouse Suites are the most opulent ever seen on a P&O cruise ship and cover two decks with large windows giving exceptional views over the bow. (P&O Cruises)*

PENTHOUSES

Entering the Suite grade of cabin, customers follow the sweep of the hall into the living area where they can appreciate the rich use of warm woods as a throwback to the traditional ships of P&O's past and where light oak or cherry wood is used in alternate cabins. The generous proportions of these areas are further enhanced by an airiness that is created by the sliding glass partitions on either side, one leading to the balcony, the other to the bedroom. Each suite has about 500 square feet of space which is over three times the size of a regular cabin and considerably larger than most hotel rooms. Furnishings

include a sofa, two armchairs and an occasional table that sits next to the sliding door leading onto the balcony. There is also a private bar and an exceptional butler service is readily available 24 hours a day. Each one has been named after a previous P&O ship such as the Chusan Suite or the Himalaya Suite with eight cabins in total on both ships all sharing the same name. The *Aurora* has an additional two cabins of this grade bringing her total up to ten cabins.

On the *Aurora* there is a very special grade of cabin which really does represent the very best in luxurious living accommodation at sea. At the forward end of Deck 10 can be found two Penthouse Suites which simply take

Above left: The Mini Suites on both ships are luxuriously appointed and cover a generous 400 square feet of room with a large private balcony. (P&O Cruises).

*Above: The upper floor of the **Aurora**'s Penthouse Suites features a large Queen Size bed, a private bathroom and a second balcony. (Brian D. Smith)*

Left: Additional features of the top grade of cabin include a private bar, a dining area served by your own butler and the best views out to sea over the ship's bow. (Brian D. Smith)

the cruise experience into another dimension. Over two decks and connected by an elegant spiral staircase, the Penthouses are each named after a unique distinct feature, the Library Suite and the Piano Suite. The Piano Suite is decorated in warm crimson and aqua tones whilst the Library Suite is furnished in mellow apricot and gold. Entering on the lower deck you cross the parquet floored entrance to the living area where to one side is the guest's cloakroom and to the other a private bar.

Overlooking the front of the ship are three double-height windows with verdant planters and a private balcony. There is an L-shaped settee where customers can enjoy the stunning views or watch the large TV, enjoy a DVD from the private collection or listen to music on the cabin's own sound system. There is even a private dining area where they can enjoy an enhanced room service menu served to you by their own private butler. The Library Suite has a reclining chair fitted with audio facilities for the many audio compact discs that are on display whilst the Piano Suite has a baby grand piano which can play itself. On the upper deck of each penthouse is a luxurious open plan bedroom with its own private balcony and views through the large forward facing windows. Luxuriously finished in porcelain and polished granite, the bathroom has twin basins, a whirlpool bath and separate shower unit whilst the walk-in wardrobe includes ironing facilities and a trouser press.

With almost 900 square feet of space these two cabins are without doubt the most spacious and luxurious cabins ever seen on a P&O Cruises ship. In total the *Aurora* has 939 cabins with the number adapted for use by disabled people significantly increased to 22.

ON-BOARD ART

There is a vast amount of British art on board both ships and P&O Cruises appointed fine art consultant Tom Tempest-Radford and sculptor Philomena Davidson Davis to advise on the art works that were to be displayed in the public areas. Paintings by artists including Janet Shearer and David Hiscock and sculptures by John Mills and James Butler fill the passenger spaces to combine with natural light and high-quality soft furnishings to really set the feel of British luxury. David Dingle said at the time of the *Oriana*'s construction, "Rather than displaying pictures and sculptures simply to fit a space or a theme as an interior decorator might, we are collecting art which will be in complete harmony with the ship and provide a source of interest and pleasure for our passengers." He continued, "Not only are existing works by British artists being sought but new sculptures and pictures are being commissioned from artists who P&O believes will be well known for

many years to come."

A total of seven different British sculptures were used on the ships and their work can be seen and appreciated in every area from John Mills' magnificent work in the *Aurora*'s atrium to the Crystal Pool where Allan Sly's pearl diver cast in bronze is carefully balanced so that he looks weightless. Between them the *Oriana* and the *Aurora* have over 6,000 paintings on display, including at least two in every cabin. The brief for Mr Tempest-Radford was to find and select works of art but not to put undue emphasis on the maritime heritage of P&O. That is why although there are paintings and models depicting various P&O ships on board, they do not predominate. He explains, "The secret of a well-displayed art collection is to hang to the available wall space. This involves taking account of every single light switch and fitting, which I had to check on the architect's plans." The idea of any art is to bring pleasure and an air of sophistication to passengers whilst they cruise. With P&O Cruises' longer than average holidays, passengers also have the time and leisure to appreciate the works chosen by the company and as you walk around the *Oriana* and *Aurora*, it is clear that those charged with this interesting venture have achieved this admirably. In fact as you walk around the *Oriana* or the *Aurora* you can see that everyone involved with designing the ship to suit the tastes of the travelling British public have done very well indeed. Anything else just wouldn't be British.

*The **Oriana** outward bound from Gibraltar during one of her Mediterranean cruises in 2010. (FotoFlite)*

*Another view of the **Aurora**'s fine atrium showing the marble pillars which strengthen in colour as they rise through the ship's decks. (Brian D. Smith)*

PICCADILLY

Aurora & Oriana

Meet Your P&O Cruises Crew

During the course of preparation for this book, the writer was extremely privileged in that P&O Cruises kindly gave him permission to speak to some of the many people who work on board the *Aurora* and the *Oriana* so that he could ascertain exactly what it is that they all do to make the cruise experience so special. The fact that so many members of the crew volunteered to speak to him was an indication of how many of them were passionate about their jobs and wanted to share with the reader their memories and experiences. All of them took great pride in telling the writer how proud they were to work for P&O Cruises and for many it was a crowning glory in what for them had been an extensive and fascinating career.

In this chapter the writer has let the crews do the talking and has simply listened to what they had to say and let them give their account in their own words. It gives him great pleasure to introduce just some of the many wonderful people that work for P&O Cruises and make it their daily responsibility to provide the best holiday anywhere in the world.

Position: Captain
Name: Neil Turnbull
Age: 45
Country of birth: United Kingdom
Date joined P&O Cruises: October 1997
Date joined the *Aurora*: March 2000
Previous P&O ships: *Canberra, Victoria, Oriana, Oceana* and the *Arcadia*

Captain Neil Turnbull was born in Carlisle before moving to Lancashire when he was seven years old. He decided in his early teens that he had a passion for the sea and after completing his formal education at Chorley in Lancashire, he went to Fleetwood Nautical College studying Marine Sciences. On completing his education at the age of 18 in 1983, he then went and worked for Pacific Nuclear Transport Limited as a deck cadet. He spent his first 15 years at sea on worldwide trading routes working on a variety of cargo, tanker and container ships rising

Captain Neil Turnbull on the bridge of the Aurora. (Brian D. Smith).

through the ranks of cadet, Third Officer and Second Officer before moving to and attaining the rank of Chief Officer on high-speed passenger ferries. Whilst working for Norse Irish Ferries and Sally Line, Neil studied at Liverpool University passing his Class 1 Certificate of Competency at Masters Level in 1994. One of his first jobs after fully qualifying as a Master was for Stena Line working on their High Speed Ship service to Ireland. Neil joined P&O Cruises in 1997 and has served on a number of ships including some from her sister company Princess Cruises. Whilst serving on the *Victoria*, he met his future wife Jayne and they have since set up home in Derbyshire. When not at sea he enjoys nothing more than spending time with his wife and their four young children Ben, Luke, Jack and Charlotte.

Describe a typical 24 hours aboard the Aurora:

There is no such thing as a typical day in the life of the Captain of *Aurora* which is what makes it the best job in the world. Life in command is of course very much dictated by the dynamics of weather, schedule, itinerary, operations as well as the more normal aspects one would consider as being inherent with any senior management role ashore and the usual demands of being responsible for the safety, welfare, morale and well-being of almost 3,000 people. Of course the prime and overriding function of a Captain is the safe navigation of his ship. Equally important is the security, health and welfare of the people on board. I am also responsible for the environmental aspects of the ship and of course the success of its commercial operation. I prefer to look upon it as being paid to take people on holiday, a job which is not only extremely challenging but extremely rewarding as well. I will now try and give you an itinerary of what I do in a 24-hour period whilst we are at sea.

07.00: Debrief from the navigator on the ship's performance overnight. We discuss any overnight issues that occurred on the ship and the day's predicted weather conditions.

Top: **The Aurora** *is dwarfed by the mountainous cliffs of the Montenegro UNESCO world heritage site at Kotor. (P&O Cruises)*

Above: **The Aurora** *makes an afternoon stop in Gibraltar on her way home from a Mediterranean cruise in October 2007. (Brian D. Smith)*

Right: *In 2004 the* **Oriana** *is seen at the Aegean Sea resort of Kusadasi. (William Mayes)*

07.30: Check e-mails received overnight and review the Hotel and Security Managers' nightly reports. Check latest weather forecasts and any potential impact on the ship's routing and/or schedule.

08.00: On the bridge to verify and confirm the ship's route, course and speed and estimated time of arrival (ETA) for the next port. I also undertake a fuller debrief with the navigator on any overnight issues.

08.30: Walk round of upper passenger decks to conduct a visual inspection and assessment of the pools and passenger areas as well as the weather conditions on the open decks. I always take this opportunity to chat with

passengers who are up before breakfast. I also meet with the crew who are on duty to see how things are going.

10.00: I do the daily public address to all the passenger areas (but not the cabins) advising information on routing for the day, expected weather and schedule for the passing of any interesting landmarks or sights we may see during the day. Afterwards, I respond to any e-mails that need actioning and progress any reports that need attention.

11.00: chair a meeting with the on-board executive team to discuss any management or departmental issues and passenger activity/reactions or requests.

*Above left: Captain Neil Turnbull with his team of Deck Officers on the bridge of the **Aurora**. (Brian D. Smith)*

*Left: The **Aurora** was the first P&O ship to have a fully enclosed bridge which was met with great approval from her Officers. Her navigation and propulsion equipment are state of the art. (Brian D. Smith)*

*Above: At 78 degrees North, Ny-Alesund is one of the world's most northernmost settlements where the temperature hardly ever goes above freezing. The **Aurora** is in the Svalbard archipelago on a glass-like sea. (P&O Cruises)*

12.00: Lunch and some rest time.

14.00: Back on the bridge to verify and confirm our course and speed as well as checking that our arrival at the next port has not changed. I will also update myself with the latest weather reports.

14.15: Walk round of lower decks, where the crew areas are, for a visual inspection. I think it is important to interact and spend time with the teams and discuss particular issues, especially those involving morale and welfare.

16.00: Conduct any Weddings or Renewal of Vows that have been booked by the passengers.

16.45: Respond to and action e-mails received and progress any reports or project work.

18.00: This is the time to put on my best uniform and to attend any social functions that we are providing for the passengers. This can go on until I host the second sitting of the evening meal in one of the main restaurants. However, I always take time out to walk around the upper decks again and carry out another visual inspection of the pools and other passenger facilities.

22.00: Final walk round of the upper passenger decks and courtesy visit of the entertainment venues in the main passenger areas.

*Their beautifully raked sterns are one of the reasons that the **Aurora** and the **Oriana** have such graceful outlines. Instantly recognisable anywhere in the world they are the epitome of what great cruise ships should look like. (P&O Cruises)*

23.00: Final visit to bridge to confirm the ship's course and speed and ETA at our next destination. I give the weather reports a review before discussing with the Senior Officer of the watch our overnight routing and speeds. I write and issue night orders and instructions for the bridge team before retiring for the night

23.15: Pyjamas on and bedtime.

Position: Executive Purser
Name: Chris Bullen
Age: 61
Country of birth: United Kingdom
Date joined P&O Cruises: August 1971
Date joined the *Oriana*: February 1995
Previous P&O ships including Princess Cruises and the British India Company: *Chusan*, *Nevasa*, *Oronsay*, *Uganda*, the original and current *Arcadia*, *Sun Princess*, *Pacific Princess*, *Sea Princess* (later P&O's *Victoria*), the original and current *Oriana*, *Canberra*, *Aurora* and the *Oceana*

Chris Bullen was born in the small Monmouthshire village of Crick and went to Larkfield Grammar School in Chepstow. Until then he had not really shown any interest in the sea but at the end of his education he joined a three-year hotel management course after having thoughts of a sea-going career awakened by visiting the *Empress of Canada* berthed in Liverpool. During his course, Chris wrote to all the well-known shipping companies in the hope that one of them would offer him a job interview. His big break came in 1971 when both the Union Castle Line and P&O offered him positions, Union Castle as a Junior Assistant Purser and P&O as a Purser Cadet. He decided to go with P&O because they had more ships than Union Castle and, therefore in Chris' eyes, there would be more chance of promotion in an ongoing career. Chris' choice proved to be the right one as in 2012 he is still with the company and has risen through the ranks to Executive Purser which he achieved back on the *Canberra* in 1992.

Executive Purser Chris Bullen. (P&O Cruises)

Describe a typical 24 hours aboard the Oriana:

I would say there is no such thing as a 'typical' day for an Executive Purser and this has been one of the advantages of working on cruise ships for the past 40 years. However, I shall try and explain some of the duties involved in running the floating 'hotel' on a daily basis. I have a team of over 650 on the *Oriana*, encompassing the hotel, entertainment and medical sections and all of them are dedicated to ensuring our passengers experience the holiday of a lifetime. So even though I head up the majority of crew on board, I am able to call on a vast array of differing expertise in the day-to-day running of the operation.

Unless we have an early port arrival I do not have a set time of starting work but I generally aim to be around between 07.30 and 08.00. I start the day by checking on the incoming e-mails, various electronic logs and hotel financial results from the day before. This is followed with a walk around the passenger public areas checking on cleanliness and general layout to ensure the ship is presented correctly for our passengers to enjoy. During this early morning walkabout I take the opportunity to call in on the Food & Beverage Manager, the Passenger Services Manager, the Finance Controller, the Commercial Manager and the Cruise Director which gives me the opportunity to chat about the previous day's events and to work out any queries that may have arisen. I will touch base with the medical team later in the day.

My breakfast time varies but I always try and eat in one of the passenger outlets whether it be the Pacific Restaurant, Al Frescos or the Conservatory as I believe in 'taking the passenger journey' as often as possible. After breakfast it's time to call in on the Captain to let him know if there are any issues in the world of 'hotel' and 'entertainment' and then back to my office for the inevitable catch-up on more e-mails and a certain amount of paperwork, some of which is electronic such as checking and authorising stores orders and some which requires an old-fashioned signature on a piece of paper such as authorising applications for crew leave swaps, requests for compassionate leave and

In 1972 P&O sent Chris Bullen with all its other cadets to the Royal Navy's training establishment HMS Royal Arthur in Corsham, Wiltshire. (Chris Bullen collection)

requests for holiday travel on board – these being merely a few examples. There may be some disciplinary issues that require some input from myself but these are thankfully very few.

Come mid-morning I would generally be involved in one of the following rounds such as checking on the standards of passenger cabin housekeeping and upkeep, similarly for crew accommodation, public area rounds or hygiene rounds of all galleys, food preparation and service areas, storerooms and bars. On occasions I will have the odd meeting to attend, for example with the Captain, the Deputy Captain and the Chief Engineer to discuss how the cruise is going and any departmental challenges that may be affecting the cruise. We also have a meeting to choose the ship's employee of the month.

If we are on a cruise that involves complicated immigration procedures, such as an arrival at a United States of America port then it is always beneficial to have a meeting to discuss the necessary requirements and to plan how we are going to make the process as easy as we can for the passengers. Arrivals in US ports are particularly challenging and give rise to issues that need plenty of prior planning and discussion.

It's now approaching lunchtime but again I have no set time and let other events dictate when I eat. Once a cruise or sometimes twice (depending on the number of passengers) I attend a Peninsular Club lunch, the special

meal held for our most loyal passengers. This gives me the chance to chat to the regular passengers and indeed this gives them the chance to ask questions of which they always have many. These lunches are extremely popular and both the crew and the passengers look forward to them.

The afternoons tend to be quieter than the mornings and so I take the opportunity to walk around the outside decks as this gives me the chance to stop and chat to some of the passengers. This is also the time to move forward with some longer-term projects and planning or to concentrate on officer appraisals. If feeling a bit peckish, I might well visit Afternoon Teas and this in turn enables me to monitor the passenger service standards.

There could well be some pre-dinner official cocktail parties such as Welcome Aboard Gala Parties or the Peninsular Club Parties to attend to and I would generally be welcoming passengers on one of the venue entrance doors. There may be a private party organised by a passenger and the occasional personal invite just might have arrived on my desk. Then it's off to dinner, again in a passenger restaurant such as one of the main restaurants or Al Frescos, the Conservatory or one of our two alternative dining outlets such as the Terrace Grill. After dinner it's a walk around to look at the entertainment on offer and eventually it's time to relax before drifting into a well-earned sleep.

Days in port frequently alter the basic routine and I must admit I have been known to be persuaded that a nice lunch ashore would be the very thing to recharge the batteries. This can be most relaxing and extremely rewarding and one of the many reasons that I enjoy working for P&O Cruises so much. I have had a wonderful career with the company and I have enjoyed every minute of it.

Ship: *Aurora* Position: Chief Engineer
Name: William Robinson
Age: 55
Country of birth: United Kingdom
Date joined P&O Cruises: February 2011
Date joined the *Aurora*: February 2011
Previous P&O ship: *Arcadia*

William Robinson knew from a very early age that he wanted a career at sea. His father was in the Royal Navy and every year took William down to Southsea in Hampshire where he used to watch all the large passenger ships using Southampton. In 1970, he saw an advert in the 'Daily Mail' to work with Shell Tankers. He responded and got a job as a cadet where he was based in South Shields. After basic training, his first vessel was the SS *Gadinia* which he joined in Japan. He spent the next 12 years with the company, working his way up the ranks until in 1984 he undertook a two-year Bachelor of Education Degree in Technology followed by three years of teaching Craft Design and Technology in secondary schools in the North East.

After five years on land, William realised that his future lay at sea and so in November 1989 he joined Cunard and served as a Junior Engineer on the 'QE2'. After only two years he took his Combined Chief Engineer's Certificate of Competency and finally reached the rank of Chief Engineer in 2002. William served on the 'QE2' for 18 years until he left the ship to go and join the *Queen Victoria* whilst she was still under construction at the Italian shipyard of Fincantieri. He remained with the ship until being transferred to P&O Cruises in February 2011 where after a very short stint on the *Arcadia* he joined the

Aurora. When not on the *Aurora* William lives in Spain with his wife where they spend much time enjoying the warm sunshine.

Describe a typical 24 hours aboard the Aurora:

I start the day at 06.00 with a call to the bridge to discuss with the navigator the progress the ship has made during the night. We generally talk about speeds required, distance, weather conditions and any requirements for the day. We will also discuss any planned maintenance we have, especially if we need to isolate any of the engines for a period of time. Next I call into the engine control room and discuss progress made during the night with Senior Second Engineer. He will raise any plant or hotel problems experienced and any work planned for that day. I scrutinise all logs before meeting briefly with Staff Chief Engineer to discuss any immediate technical problems experienced during the night. Once this is done I read my e-mails and compose a list of items to discuss at the daily technical meeting which starts at 07.30 each day. I will also complete all my daily logs regarding fuel and water consumption, check the maintenance record database (AMOS) for any outstanding work and check all the technical store orders that are awaiting my approval.

Afterwards I hold a meeting with senior technical staff to discuss any work that is to be carried out in the various departments as well as any environmental issues that have arisen. Normally all this is completed by 08.00 and so all staff can carry out their duties or planned maintenance for the day.

The rest of the day consists of answering e-mails and technical inspections in the engine room spaces and the rest of the ship. I will later attend various inter-departmental meetings such as the crew rounds and the public health rounds before gathering information for the noon fuel logs where I monitor the ship's performance and fuel consumption. There is also some report writing to be done on the various aspects of the technical department which requires updating on a daily or weekly basis. I meet regularly with other department heads to discuss any problems and

Chief Engineer William Robinson. (Brian D. Smith)

*Top left: One of the **Aurora**'s four M.A.N diesel engines generating 14,400 kw of energy. This is then transformed into electrical energy before powering the ship. (Brian D. Smith)*

*Top right: Staff Chief Engineer Luke Sheldon checks the oil mist detector on one of the **Aurora**'s main engines. (Brian D. Smith)*

Above: Engineering is fun, just ask Ernesto Contado Jr and Ariel Maling as they change a cam follower. (Brian D. Smith)

*Right: William Robinson stands on one of the **Aurora**'s main engines to give a sense of scale. He could fit inside one of the 14 cylinders with room to spare. (Brian D. Smith)*

what is going well and not so well so that we can quickly identify any challenges coming our way.

On some afternoons I attend one of the Portunus lunches which are held in one of the main restaurants. This gives me the opportunity to meet some of our regular passengers and answer their many questions about the ship. I will also attend various cocktail parties which take place in the evening. Later in the afternoon, I view all the engine room spaces and discuss with all watch keepers any problems we may be having. I spend some time with the technical stores manager to discuss what spares are required and how the ship's technical finances are

progressing. My normal working day can finish around 19.00 but I am on call 24 hours a day to assist where necessary.

On a port day everything I have just told you takes place but for me the day generally starts much earlier as I need to be in the engine control room for all arrival standbys. This is usually 15 minutes or so before the pilot arrives and then I should remain on standby with the watch keepers until the ship is safely tied up alongside. Prior to departure I need to check with my senior team that any repairs or maintenance carried out during our stay in port has been completed and that the plant is

*Above left: Just three years after entering service, the **Oriana** is seen at the old Norwegian Capital of Trondheim where it never gets dark in the month of June. (William Mayes)*

*Left: The bow of the **Oriana** is seen by one of the many bridges in Venice close to the entrance of the Grand Canal. (P&O Cruises).*

*Above: The snow-topped Norwegian Fjords make a dramatic background to the **Oriana** as she sails in Sognefjord which is the second largest of all the Fjords. (P&O Cruises)*

ready for sea-going conditions. I have to attend the bridge at least 30 minutes before standby for departure to give a positive written safety and technical report that confirms that we are ready to leave. I am then positioned on the bridge whilst the ship leaves the berth and normally until the pilot leaves and the ship rings full away. My position in the engine control room is covered by the Staff Chief Engineer, my right hand man and immediate deputy. During my time on the bridge for standby, the ship's speed and engine configurations are planned for the next leg of the cruise as well as discussing any relevant maintenance issues. Once the ship is away to sea, I leave the bridge and

confirm that the engines and plant are settled ready for the next leg of the cruise.

Of course, any day in our turnaround port of Southampton is a very busy period. Things like fuel bunkering and sludge discharge are all areas where I need to keep a very watchful eye as I am responsible for all these and other various operations which we need to undertake and they must run smoothly and safely. In various ports we may be subject to the World Health inspections or Port State Control inspections as well as the usual safety annual and quarterly checks carried out by the United States Coastguard and the Maritime Coastguard

*The **Norway** is seen behind the **Oriana** as she waits for her lifeboats to come back from refit at the German shipyard of Lloyd Werft. (Lloyd Werft)*

Agency in the UK. This can involve a great many hours demonstrating to auditors and inspectors that the ship and its systems and practices strictly adhere to all the rules guidelines and regulations laid out in various international rules and documents. As you can imagine all P&O Cruises ships are maintained to the very highest standards and we never have any real issues passing even the toughest of tests set out by the various regulatory bodies.

Ship: *Oriana*   Position: Executive Chef
Name: Carl Withers
Age: 48
Country of birth: United Kingdom
Date joined P&O Cruises: November 2000
Date joined the *Oriana*: March 2010
Previous P&O ships: The second *Arcadia*, the first *Adonia*, *Artemis* and the *Aurora*

Carl Withers was born in Stratford upon Avon in Warwickshire. Throughout his education he had a desire to work in the catering industry so when he left school in 1980, he started his Chef's apprenticeship at the local Hilton International where he worked and studied for the next three years. Upon becoming a Commis Chef he transferred to the Hilton at Gatwick Airport where he served for less than a year before transferring to the Hilton in Amsterdam, Holland. He clearly had a taste (no pun intended) for foreign travel so after he had finished working in Holland he went and worked at the White Sands Hotel in Bermuda as the Chef De Partie. Carl has also worked in New Zealand and Hong Kong where in

1990 his culinary expertise allowed him to apply for the role of Sous Chef at the famous Jimmy's Kitchen on the Peak and then The Aberdeen Marina Club, a five star members club managed by Shangri-la hotels. After over ten years of travelling, Carl returned to work in the UK where he finally achieved his ambition of becoming a Head Chef at the Alverston Manor Hotel in 1997.

Of course Carl had the travel bug and could not sit still for long. So in 2000 he joined P&O Cruises where his undoubted talent and flair for cooking was soon recognised resulting in him being given the position of Executive Chef aboard the *Aurora* in 2008.

When not working at sea Carl likes nothing more than spending time with his family back in Warwickshire or on holiday in the Philippines.

Describe a typical 24 hours aboard the Oriana:

I start the day at 07.00 after checking my e-mails and daily report from the previous dinner. I then do the rounds of the galley areas from Deck 12 downwards as they are already open for breakfast. I liaise with the night chef to see if anything has happened during the night which might affect the restaurants during the day. Before going downstairs I will have a quick look at the Conservatory Buffet to ensure everything is available and in its best condition for our passengers. I will meet the Sous Chef responsible for the Conservatory and enquire whether all is how it should be regarding both the product and staffing.

Then it's back to the main galley on Deck 6 where the Senior Sous Chef is ready to start breakfast in the Peninsular Restaurant. It is his responsibility to bring to my attention any shortages of product, any equipment repairs or any other issues that he thinks I need to know about. I then visit the crew galley and the prep rooms to see what is going on there. Feeding the crew is just as important as feeding the passengers and it is my responsibility to make sure that everything runs smoothly.

At around 08.30 it is coffee time before I speak with the various members of staff who are responsible for the different types of food which we are going to serve during the day. At least two days' menus will be discussed and this includes an input from the Food Store Keeper to make sure that we are using up food that is approaching its best before date or to make sure we are using anything that we

Executive Chef Carl Withers. (P&O Cruises)

reports from the previous day and to clarify the planned day's events such as a private luncheon or a Peninsular Club lunch. We discuss what will happen if we are having a BBQ on the Lido Deck and it rains. We make sure that any birthday cakes due at the dinner service are ready for collection later that day and we also discuss any problems that the passengers have raised such as food not being hot enough or alternatively not cold enough and what we can do to stop this from happening again. Once this is completed I visit the alternative restaurants such as the Marco Pierre White's Ocean Grill at the Curzon Room restaurant on Deck 8

may have plenty of stock of. It is at this point that I normally find out if we have any shortages or are over stocked in any areas. If necessary I will make any required changes to the corporate menu cycle before the amounts for fish and meat are finalised and their stores chit signed or adjusted.

Once my team have agreed on the day's food it is off to the printers with the draft menus. Once the printers have completed them, I then proof read everything before passing them to the Deputy Food and Beverage Manager who also proof reads the menus before the wine offering for the day is selected. Once this has been agreed the new menu is then passed back to the printers, ready for the lunch and dinner service later that day. When this is done, I liaise with the Premier Sous Chef who is responsible for the day-to-day running of the galley. We then visit the various section heads who can let us know if there are any problems with the menus we have just selected. By 09.30, I need to approve all the food order chits so that the necessary food can be released from the stores. For me, I have to balance the needs of the various department heads who require a certain amount of food so that they can complete the menu to the required standard but remain within budget whilst making sure that I do not use up too much food that we run out of a particular item. As long as there is regular communication between everyone this should never happen.

Breakfast is normally over by now and so I meet with the two Senior Restaurant Managers to discuss their

to see how many are booked in for dinner that night and to see if they are fully staffed and fully prepared for the dinner service later that night. Then I will call in to see the Food and Beverage Manager in his office (hopefully with an invitation for coffee) to discuss just about anything involved in the catering department such as current issues or trends and to raise suggestions and plan departmental meetings.

The crew mess opens at 11.00 which is checked by the duty Sous Chef, followed by the Officers' Mess at 11.30. Once again, if any problems cannot be resolved by the Sous Chef, he will bring them to me so that they can be sorted out immediately before the rush for lunch starts (remember some of the crew will have been up from a very early hour and can't wait for their lunch).

The passengers' lunch is the first main meal of the day and the Galley Management Team and I will view and taste all the food being offered for that serving. This allows us to make any final adjustments before the food is served. During the lunch I will be on hand doing what I call periodic walkabouts offering advice and assistance where it is needed.

Lunch normally finishes around 13.30 and the Afternoon Teas are looked after by the Duty Sous Chef. This gives me some time off as I am not back on duty until 17.00. Just as with lunch I will speak to all the various heads and restaurant managers to make sure everything is as it should be. The staff on the *Oriana* are very good at their jobs, which makes my life that little bit easier. I do the same thing with the conservatory theme buffet which opens at 18.00 after which it is all hands to the pumps to make sure that the evening meal is presented in the exemplary fashion that people rightly expect of P&O Cruises. During the evening meal I will monitor the service line or carve the evening roast if necessary, while the Senior Sous Chef collates the count to ensure we have enough of the product after first sitting to complete the second sitting. If necessary I can arrange any emergency orders that may be required but thankfully this does not happen very often. The second sitting is normally over by about 22.00 when we are busy cleaning down the galleys and restaurants ready to do it all again the following day. I then clean my inbox of any e-mails, double-check the daily food issues and relevant costs before calling it a day around 22.30. I then handover to the night team who are on hand to attend to any food requirements that the passengers may have during the night.

Working on the *Oriana* is truly a 24-hour operation where you have to be ready to deal with the unexpected. Turning out meals for over 2,500 people is a great achievement and to do it to the standard expected of our passengers is a really rewarding experience. The *Oriana* is a great place to live and to work which I love and wouldn't change for anything.

Ship: *Oriana*   **Position:** Chief Security Officer
Name: Graham Russell
Age: 57
Country of birth: United Kingdom
Date joined P&O Cruises: January 2007
Date joined the *Oriana*: My first time was March 2008
Previous P&O ships: All current ships of the P&O Cruises fleet

Graham Russell was born in Aldershot Hampshire, the home of the British Army. He attended St Michael's Primary School just along from the Recreation Ground, home to Aldershot Football Club, which he still supports. The sea has always been a satisfying place and weekend day trips to the south coast during the summer months of Graham's younger years were a regular event. Watching through plastic binoculars the ships of the past, such as the *Queen Mary* and the *Queen Elizabeth* leaving Southampton and disappearing past the Nab

Tower are treasured memories. After progressing to senior school at St Michael's he left and started an engineering apprenticeship with a local firm before moving to Marconi Space and Defence Systems. On completion of his apprenticeship he joined the Hampshire Constabulary and never looked back. The challenges that frontline policing offered provided for a wonderful career which he is very proud of. On joining P&O Cruises he has managed to utilise his skills and expertise from the police force in his role as the Chief Security Officer. Whilst on leave, Graham loves to spend time at home, either in the New Forest or in Spain with his wife Marilyn, their son and daughter and their grandchildren.

Describe a typical 24 hours aboard the Oriana:

How my day starts is really decided by the ship's itinerary and, just like police work, what the passengers and crew get up to. If arrival in a port is before 06.00 hours I would be up and about a good hour or so before. If it is a sea day then I would be in the office about 06.30. Prior to going to my office, I visit the security team to see how they are and catch up on anything that has happened. We talk about the day ahead and discuss matters such as how best the gangways would run, medical disembarkations and any visitors for the day. If passes have not been printed the day before, I will then go to the office and print them.

One of my team would have completed both fire and safety rounds during the night and the Night Manager would have completed a Hotel Night Log. The rounds identify defects and safety issues which are then discussed

with the ship's Safety Officer. Anything specific I will discuss with the Deputy Captain, identifying options and what course of action may be appropriate. Looking through e-mails and post that has arrived overnight provides replies to pre-arrival questionnaires regarding the security particulars of the ports that the ship will visit. The pre-arrival information is forwarded at least 72 hours prior to arrival and is a condition of the ISPS Code of Practice that defines procedures that we have to follow. The correspondence has to be completed and questions answered or entry to the port would be refused. If the security level

Chief Security Officer Graham Russell. (P&O Cruises)

of the port has been raised due to current or historical events then planning for additional security measures has to be completed and the measures put in place before arrival in port. This time of the morning is quiet and allows for much of the pending paperwork to be completed before the busy part of the day gets under way. A cup of tea and a visit to the bridge to see where we are and to view the night log is normally next on my agenda. This is because the bridge is the control centre of all incidents which occur on board the ship.

It may be appropriate for an early morning call to a passenger or crew member as I am responsible for investigations into accidents and other incidents on board and this is where my previous career knowledge comes in. Checking with cabin stewards usually identifies who is about and the likelihood of maybe a short interview before arrival in port as the passengers will be away on tours and visits; after all they are on holiday! The *Oriana* is like a small village with shops, restaurants and various entertainment venues, including betting and alcohol recreational areas which can lead to issues. Should something serious occur then the Security Team would set up a crime scene and evidence would be preserved in the usual manner. An investigation would commence and, if necessary, would be handed over to local law enforcement agencies. The purpose of this is to give the authorities the best opportunity to investigate the matter and have evidence lawfully obtained that would stand the test if presented in a court of law. I am also responsible for monitoring the ship's CCTV system and ensuring any relevant footage is available for evidence.

Once in port I ensure the teams are setting up the security equipment, including the access control computers, podiums and scanning equipment which has to be calibrated on every occasion. Sometimes gangway brows have to be changed and turned around from port to starboard side; this is something the coxswains do and we assist when necessary. A last minute change of plan by changing deck or side to the quay means everything is dismantled and moved to the new location ready for the command from the bridge to open the shell doors. When the ship is alongside and the gangways landed or air bridge accepted, I leave the ship to speak with the official party. This can range from the ship's agent to the local police, customs, immigration, port health, US coastguard or the harbour master. Once the official party is on board I will conduct a quayside inspection regarding both security of the facility and safety regarding coaches for tours, parking access to the quayside and slip and trip hazards. If available I will speak with the Port Facility Security Officer. They are usually responsible for completing the pre-arrival security documents on behalf of the port and can provide an update on local issues. I would then report information to the bridge in preparation for a formal announcement to

be made once clearance is given and passengers may then disembark.

I remain for the initial rush of passengers ensuring that everything is functioning properly and deal with any identified issues. When things have quietened down, I will check the stores and bunker areas especially if doors are open to ensure that the shell door logs are completed and the door sentry is alright and carrying out their duties. If it is early in the cruise I may have to deliver the security brief to new crew members, or take part in a full crew drill.

My day continues with future cruise port planning and preparing pre-arrival paperwork. This is often interrupted by passenger or crew-related incidents from minor crime matters to accidents. Medical emergencies on board require attendance to ensure routes are clear back to the Medical Centre and also to close down an area to keep persons away. During the afternoon I may attend a Peninsular Club Lunch or other social function which gives me the chance to meet and interact with passengers on a less formal basis and this is something that I enjoy very much. Afterwards, I will walk all areas of the ship talking to passengers and crew alike, keeping up to date with what is happening and observing any developing trends that may be occurring.

Team training takes place on a regular basis with classroom sessions, role-play and tabletop exercises to ensure new regulations are introduced and skills maintained. During sea days I monitor the maintenance programme for all of the security equipment and where necessary make arrangements to have it repaired.

Nearing the end of a port call we await the returning tours of the crew and passengers and then, when numbers of persons outstanding are manageable with one gangway, we start to remove furniture and barriers used during the visit from the quayside. This is timed so that everything is clear ready to embark the pilot and so after ensuring that everyone is on board and visitors are all ashore, we remove the final gangway. Once the ship departs, a patrol to ensure things are secure, that no one is hiding in lifeboats and the like, are carried out. I then return to the office to finish off any incomplete paperwork and tidy up and clear as much as I can so that I have a clean start the following day.

Days prior to turnaround are particularly busy with the administration of joiners and leavers and visitors' passes lists amounting to hundreds of people. At any time in port we may be subject to an inspection by the Port State Control or the Coastguard to mention but two. This can mean a lengthy time demonstrating that P&O Cruises work to the legislation and codes of practice required and maintain the highest of standards expected of us by ourselves and our passengers.

Ship: *Aurora*   Position: Restaurant Manager
Name: Alan Carr
Country of birth: United Kingdom
Date joined P&O Cruises: February 1995
Date joined the *Aurora*: May 2010
Previous P&O ships: *Oriana*, *Oceana*, *Ventura*, *Victoria*, *Artemis* and the third *Arcadia*

Restaurant Manager Alan Carr. (Brian D. Smith)

Alan Carr grew up in the lovely Lancashire town of Tyldesley where he lived with his twin sister Pat and their foster mother Carolyn. Alan credits her with everything he has achieved in life and holds her in the highest regard. When Alan finished school he started his career at sea by joining the Royal Navy working in the catering department. As there were no chef-related jobs available, he started as a Junior Steward Second Class. Over the next few years he served on a number of different ships including HMS *Ajax*, HMS *Brilliant* and HMS *Jupiter*. He even served on HMS *Aurora* as a Petty Officer Steward, which makes his connection with his present ship just that little bit more special. Alan's last ship in the Senior Service was HMS *Cornwall* which he left in 1995 to work for P&O Cruises. Despite a long career at sea, Alan reckons that at the moment he has the best job in the world. He says it is a dream job and one he loves very much. He looks forward to meeting a new set of passengers on every cruise and takes great personal pride in his work; especially when he manages to solve any problems that passengers may find during their dinner service. Watching them enjoying their time on board and leaving the ship very happy indeed is a great feeling which Alan never gets tired of. When not serving on the *Aurora*, Alan likes to keep himself fit and spend time with his grandchildren and the rest of the family.

Describe a typical 24 hours aboard the Aurora:

I normally rise about 06.30 which is due to my time in the Royal Navy; I have always been an early riser even at the age of 14 when I did a paper round. I shower and then head in to the alternative dining areas, have a cup of tea and walk the decks. I think this is the best time of the day, especially if any paperwork is required such as the morning report from the previous day, as there is nothing to disturb me while I watch the rising sun. I try and do this often and consider it one of the reasons I am so lucky to have my dream job.

As the Alexandra Restaurant is not open for breakfast, I spend the morning monitoring the service in the Orangery, the Cafe Bordeaux and the Sidewalk Café. I will also support the other restaurant manager in the Medina Restaurant if necessary. I like to chat with the passengers hoping that they are enjoying the cruise as much as I am working on it.

At 10.00 every day we have what is called a '10 at 10 meeting' with members of the restaurant team, the galley team and some of the Food and Beverage Department to discuss the previous day's menus and dinner service. Here we can iron out any issues that have arisen and give positive feedback to the members of our teams that have made recommendations to us or suggested any new bright ideas to help improve our service.

Usually, if we are in port I go for a morning run after the meeting. I will also go circuit training as I really like to stay in peak condition to do my job. Whatever I do I am always back on board and ready to start the lunch service in the areas of the ship that are to open to passengers on that day. If there are any special functions, such as the gold tier Peninsular Luncheons, then these will normally take place in the Alexandra Restaurant and I will be on duty to make sure we offer a first class service to our longest serving customers. It's just our way of thanking them for their continued support of P&O Cruises and I always enjoy these events. Every so often I am fortunate enough to have a lunch off and this is spent going ashore taking in the various sights or laying on the beach where I just go swimming and enjoy life.

After lunch at about 14.00, it is time for some well-earned rest and either a walk ashore or, if at sea, a spot of sun worshipping before returning back to work at 17.00 in preparation for the evening dinner. We hold a staff briefing at 18.10 informing all the restaurant staff of their commitments and duties for the next 24 hours. I always use this time to thank my staff for their continued hard work and the excellent service that they give the

*Overlooking the Riviera Pool on the **Aurora**. (Miles Cowsill)*

passengers. At 18.30 we have the first sitting and I make sure that all the passengers are greeted at the door before they are individually seated. Once the dinner service is under way I check with the other department heads to make sure everything is going to plan. At 20.30 we have the second sitting and again I make sure all the passengers receive the same high-quality service that I pride myself on. You have no idea how pleased I am when I walk around the restaurant and see all the passengers enjoying themselves. It really does make me proud when I think of what we have done to provide them with such a great cruise experience. Normally by about 22.30 the second dinner service is coming to an end and I usually go straight to my cabin to rest. It's not long before I am off to bed for a good night's sleep after another successful day.

Once a month we have a social gathering of all the restaurant staff in appreciation of the hard work and commitment that each and every one of them puts in to doing their job. This is a great team builder and makes for a happy working environment which, of course, cascades down to our passengers making their cruise even more enjoyable. No two days are the same in my job so I make sure that I never become complacent. My motto which I

share with my staff is that we must always be prepared for the unexpected circumstances that may arise and meet the challenges of any new day with a positive outlook.

Ship: *Oriana*   **Position:** Spa Manager
Name: Kylie McDade
Age: 24
Country of birth: United Kingdom
Date joined P&O Cruises: October 2009
Date joined the *Oriana:* June 2011
Previous P&O ship: *Oceana*

Kylie McDade was born in South Lanarkshire, Scotland. She went to school in Hamilton before going to a hairdressers' college to gain her qualifications in hair makeover. When she had completed her training she obtained a job at a local salon where she worked for the next five years. Whilst working there she met a lady who had worked aboard the *Aurora*. She had clearly enjoyed her time with P&O Cruises because she talked about it non stop and managed to convince Kylie that she too would love working on a cruise ship. Kylie contacted P&O Cruises and signed up for a one-contract period. Two years later she is still with the company and on her third contract. She has proved her worth to the company because in that short period she has been promoted twice and is now the Spa Manager. Kylie loves her job and is so pleased that she took her friend's advice and found a job at sea. She cannot imagine doing anything else and considers herself to be in a very envious position, being paid to do a job that she absolutely loves.

Describe a typical 24 hours aboard the Oriana:

As the Spa Manager I am responsible for the day-to-day running of the fitness gymnasium and the health and beauty spa. On most days this starts for my team and me at 07.45 when we have our first meeting of the day to set out the day's programme depending on what is booked into the complex. Sometimes one of the fitness instructors will help us get going with a short exercise routine which wakes us all up. After the meeting we begin to set up the health and beauty spa for the day by diffusing aromatherapy oils around the various rooms that we have here on the Oriana such as the massage rooms or the saunas. I then make sure that the massage therapists turn on the hot cabbies to warm the aroma stones, the bamboo and Thai poultices for their signature massage treatments which are very popular with our passengers. The beauty therapists will then warm the mitts and compresses, whilst preparing for their first facials of the day. By now some of the passengers have finished breakfast and are popping their heads into the spa to see where that wonderful aroma is coming from.

We open the fitness gym at 08.00, by which time there are usually more than a few passengers keen to start their early morning workout. One of the things I consider to be very important is to make sure that all of our guests are greeted with a warm and friendly smile. With the wonderfully tranquil environment that we create each and every day in the spa, I want all of our guests to have a welcoming and relaxing experience whilst with us.

Although every night is special whilst working on board the Oriana, the formal evenings are extra special as the spa is always full with ladies having their hair styled; their nails manicured and make-up applied in preparation for the

Spa Manager Kylie McDade. (Brian D Smith)

wonderful night that awaits them.

When we have a wedding on board the Oriana I make sure that the bride and her entourage are made very welcome when using our fantastic facilities. Normally the bride will bring up a bottle of champagne which she enjoys with her friends and family whilst the hairstylist fits the tiara into the intricate hairstyle they have just created. The bridesmaids are also well looked after as well as the immediate family of both the bride and groom. We give them a very professional service which normally ends with a few tears when the bride comes back to show us what she looks like in her full regalia. It is extremely satisfying to watch the wedding party all going off to the ceremony knowing that we have done our bit to make their day just that little bit extra special.

In the late afternoon the fitness gym can become very busy as passengers come in for a good workout before they go and get ready for the evening's entertainment. My fitness team offer one-to-one training programmes which are tailor made to each individual passenger's particular needs. They also offer classes such as Circuit Training or Pilates, which are very popular, or they allow people to work out at their own leisure but observe to supervise and advise where necessary.

By early evening things have started to quieten down as the last of the guests leave the salon with hair coiffed to perfection and the fitness team begin to wipe down and clean all of the equipment. Once everything is put away and the complex is shut down, I go around and make sure everything is in its place and set up for the next day. Whether it's a black tie evening on a sea day or a casual night after a day in port, there is always a lot to do in the spa and my team and I work hard to make sure we do everything that we can to give our passengers the best possible spa experience. Working for P&O Cruises on such a lovely ship is so rewarding and I love every minute of my working day. When you are on board the Oriana next, please come up to the Spa and see me. It will be a great pleasure to meet you.

Ship: *Aurora*
Position: Cruise Director
Name: Jon Bartram
Age: 45
Country of birth: United Kingdom
Date joined P&O Cruises: November 2003
Date joined the *Aurora*: November 2005
Previous P&O ships: *Oriana*, *Oceana*, *Artimus*, *Arcadia* and the original *Adonia*

Jon Bartram has trained in all aspects of theatre since he was five years old. He specialised in ballet from the age of nine and continued to develop in all aspects of entertainment whilst he was at school. Upon finishing his education he immediately went into the theatrical profession and has since performed in some of the world's most famous productions. Between 1985 and 1994 he appeared in musicals such as 'Evita', '42nd Street', 'Guys n Dolls' and a repertory season at the Redgrave Theatre in Surrey.

He also has a great love for the traditional British pantomime and has appeared in such roles as Little Jack Horner in 'Jack and the Beanstalk', one of the ugly sisters in 'Cinderella' and the genie of the lamp in 'Aladdin'. In between musicals and pantomime he has appeared in a number of plays such as 'Ladies Night', 'Twelfth Night' and 'A Street Car Named Desire'. His TV and film highlights include 'The House of Eliott' and 'The People's Princess'. He has even appeared as a double for the late Roy Castle.

In 1998 Jon set up his own production company based in Mallorca, providing shows, cabarets and popular outdoor events across Europe. He sold this in 2003 so that he could change the direction of his career. Back in 1987 Jon had a brief experience working on the *Cunard Countess* performing as a singer and a dancer. It was this that gave Jon the desire to go to sea permanently so in 2003 he joined up with P&O Cruises and started as the Entertainments Officer on the *Adonia*. He remained in this position until in 2005 he was invited to join the set up team of P&O Cruises new ship, the *Arcadia*, where he was promoted to Assistant Cruise Director. In 2005 he worked on both the *Aurora* and the *Arcadia* before being promoted to Deputy Cruise Director on the *Aurora* in November 2006 and becoming the Cruise Director a year later. In his current role, Jon has overall responsibility for delivering the

Cruise Director, John Bartram. (P&O Cruises)

entertainments programme including the theatre shows, the cabarets, the guest speakers and the tutoring and learning programme where passengers can learn such skills as dance, language and bridge. He also oversees the youth department but leaves the day-to-day running to the Youth Director.

When he is not at sea Jon enjoys walking across the Dartmoor area of Devon with fiancée Michelle, who he met on the *Oriana*, keeping a lookout for potential wedding reception venues. He is also extremely passionate about his favourite football team, Liverpool Football Club.

Describe a typical 24 hours aboard the Aurora:

I wake up by 08.00 which is a lot later than most of the crew on the ship but I also finish a lot later than they do. Within 30 minutes I have finished my first cup of strong coffee and do a brief walk of the ship. Afterwards I check my e-mails, which can be a large number, and I also make sure that I am up to date with the latest compliance, safety and legal matters which can take up until 10.00. Once this is completed I will again walk the ship attending events to see for myself how many passengers are utilising the events we arrange for them while receiving their feedback. Between 11.30 and 12.30 I am in the office completing

*Both the **Aurora** and the **Oriana** put on high-quality each night. (P&O)*

correspondence for our shore-side business and visiting my on-board colleagues for any day-to-day business; once this is completed then I can have lunch. Immediately afterwards I tour the open decks meeting with the passengers and enjoy engaging them in conversation. At about 15.00 I will go back to the office for future cruise planning.

By the late afternoon I need to attend rehearsals for the evening show or cabaret and catch up with my production team. I then get my final break of the day before my busy evening schedule starts. As the evening festivities get under way, I finalise all correspondence and action any further company business. I then host the evening's main events including both shows in the theatre (or participate) and catch up with passengers on a social walkabout. Hopefully by about midnight I have finished my duties and am ready for my bed.

Port days will normally be quieter on the passenger interaction aspect but in the mornings there will still be meetings, safety drills and staff appraisals to be completed. We still have to provide an evening's entertainment so even though the passengers are ashore enjoying themselves, the entertainments team and I are working hard to make sure that this continues when they return to the ship. Judging by the many happy faces that I see walking around the ship, I think it's something that we at P&O Cruises do rather well.

Ship: *Aurora* Position: Accommodation Service Manager
Name: Leslie Vaz
Age: 47
Country of birth: Kenya
Date joined P&O Cruises: October 1995
Date joined the *Aurora*: September 2001
Previous P&O ships: *Oriana*, *Oceana*, the original *Adonia* and the *Artemis*

Leslie Vaz was born in Nairobi, Africa but at the age of four years old, his family decided to move to Goa in India. After completing his education, he went on to university where he became very active in the sporting world, especially in cricket and football. It was whilst Leslie was studying at university that he developed a taste for travelling and so he took on the responsibility of organising

some of the excursions for students as part of their educational courses. This gave him immense satisfaction when it was reported back to him how successful these trips had been. It was whilst he was organising a trip to a five star hotel that he got drawn into the glamour and excitement of the hospitality industry and decided this is where his future lay.

When Leslie graduated from university in 1985 he took a diploma course in Hotel Management and within a few months he managed to get a job as a trainee with one of the Holiday Inn chain of hotels in Goa. He thoroughly enjoyed his work but was frustrated at the lack of opportunities to go into management so he joined the Kempinski group of hotels at the Leela. Whilst working there an old friend wrote to him telling him how much he was enjoying life now that he was working for P&O Princess Cruises. He immediately wondered what it must be like to see such wonderful destinations as America and Australia and maybe, just maybe, to fulfil a lifetime's ambition of watching a cricket match at the Oval Cricket Ground. To do all this and get paid for working in an industry that he loved would be simply surreal. He immediately applied for a job with the company and a few weeks later got an interview with a Mr Zac Coombs, now the Executive Purser on the *Adonia*. Later in October 1995 was to be one of the happiest times of Leslie's life when he was offered the job of Deck Supervisor on the *Sea Princess*, and in his own words, he hasn't looked back since.

Accommodation Services Manager Leslie Vaz. (Brian D. Smith)

During his time with the company Leslie has served on a variety of ships at various ranks but most of his time has been spent on the mighty *Aurora* which is one of his favourites.

Describe a typical 24 hours aboard the Aurora:

My day begins at about 06.30 when I read through my e-mails, check the ship's night log, (which gives me a detailed report of any accommodation problems that would have been raised during the night) and then walk around the cabin decks with the night shift supervisor to make sure that everything is as it should be for both us and the passengers. Once I have done this I stop off at the laundry to see how things are going. The laundry is a hive of activity 24 hours a day and it never stops. In here people are cleaning, ironing or folding bed linen, to name but a few of the jobs we have to do. After my daily morning rounds are over, I have a quick breakfast before returning to my desk to begin planning the day's tasks. I then hold a team briefing with all my supervisors to assign them the day's responsibilities and to receive any feedback on the previous day's activities. My day continues by co-ordinating my department's work with other departments on the ship to make sure that any defects are repaired as soon as possible and that any requirements we have for a particular passenger's needs are taken care of. I also have to work with the Furnishing Support Team back at Southampton to make sure they have all of our requirements ready for us for when we next arrive home. I have to continuously liaise with the Front of House Manager to check on any passenger requests or complaints they may have received and to do what I can to make sure that all the passengers' desires are met so that they have a really good time whilst they are on the *Aurora*. At about this time I will again walk the passenger decks to supervise the cleaning of the cabins and to support my staff as they work. I believe that by working closely with the staff that I am responsible for I can offer them the support and advice that they need whilst ensuring that the service standards set down by the company are being met.

With responsibility for over 900 cabins I have a department of around 140 personnel which means apart from supervising the work that they do, I also have to arrange their training, manage their leave requests and make sure that everyone knows their job as well as that day's responsibilities. I do this in conjunction with the Human Resources team based at Carnival House in Southampton. This, of course, is subject to my workload and can vary on a weekly, if not daily basis. Almost every day of the week my department undergoes various spot checks to make sure we are maintaining correct levels of public health and complying with the latest environmental guidelines. I also meet with passengers who are not happy with something in their cabins and wish to speak to the supervisor. With such a professional crew this hardly ever happens but when it does we can always put things right. The most important thing to me is to make sure that every passenger has an enjoyable stay whilst on the *Aurora* and if either my department or I can do anything to improve their time on board we will do it immediately and without hesitation.

If it is a port day then I may wander ashore during lunchtime for an hour or two as it's always nice to visit the many different destinations that we go to and stretch my legs a bit. If it is a sea day then I will take a break and get something to eat.

Occasionally at lunchtime and in the evenings I have

the pleasure of attending one of the Peninsular Lunches or even the evening cocktail parties before dining in one of the main passenger restaurants which helps me interact with passengers and get a feel for how they are enjoying the cruise. I always enjoy telling them about myself and what I do but the best bit is always telling them how much I love working for P&O Cruises.

Normally I am back at my desk for around 16.00 where I do my final walk of the passenger decks before finishing for the day. Before I break off for the day, I will have a quick meeting with the supervisors when they will bring to my attention any new problems that may have arisen. Then I pop into the laundry which is still going strong and will keep going right throughout the night. The last thing I do before signing off for the day is to check my e-mails and make sure that all the evening's tasks have been correctly assigned to the relevant personnel. Once this is done I get a chance to enjoy a meal with my colleagues and to unwind and relax in the Officers' Mess. Then it's off to bed for the start of another day.

Leslie Vaz working hard with the champagne bottle. (Brian D. Smith)

*The **Aurora** sailing on a beautiful blue sea with some of her passengers enjoying the warm summer sun on her outside decks. (FotoFlite)*

Aurora & Oriana

Exclusively for Adults

Since the *Oriana* first entered service back in 1995, she has provided P&O Cruises with years of loyal service, sailing over a million miles and taking thousands of passengers on holiday to destinations all over the world.

By the beginning of 2010 she was approaching her 15th birthday and around the halfway point of her service life. Although extremely well maintained, it could not be denied that compared to some of her modern stable mates, she was looking a little tired in some areas and could do with a little freshening up for the second part of her life. The company held a complete review of the ship and decided how best she could serve them whilst meeting the demands of the modern-day cruise passenger.

The demographics of these cruise passengers had changed considerably in the time the *Oriana* had been in service as had their desires and tastes. Not only were the number of families sailing with young children significantly increasing but so were the number of people who wanted a different type of cruise and were more suited to the exclusively for adults type of holiday which the company offered on only two of its ships, the *Adonia* and the *Arcadia*. With the introduction of newer and much larger family friendly ships such as the *Ventura* and the *Azura*, P&O Cruises had catered for those that desired a family holiday, but there was clearly an opportunity with the *Oriana* to increase the number of ships that were exclusively for adults and to expand the number of ships and destinations that P&O Cruises could offer those that wanted this type of holiday. The number of people who wanted to go on an exclusively for adults cruise from the United Kingdom had increased year on year for some time and future cruise predictions showed that this number was going to continue to rise for the foreseeable future.

From late 2009 and well into 2010 a series of high-level meetings were held to discuss the future of the *Oriana* and it was finally agreed that she would be converted to a ship exclusively for adults and go for a complete refit that would see her through to the end of her expected life with P&O Cruises. Engineering and propulsion systems would be upgraded as well as most of the public rooms and deck spaces along with the introduction of two new additional restaurants giving passengers the choice of an alternative dining venue which had proved to be a great success on some of the company's other ships. The children's area on Deck 8 would be removed and some additional cabins, including some much needed additional balconied cabins installed here instead. Although the *Oriana* entered service with more balconied cabins than any other British cruise ship in history, it cannot be denied that she does not have enough balconied cabins to satisfy the modern-day demand for this type of amenity and has a significantly lower percentage of balconied cabins than the rest of the P&O Cruises fleet. A new type of cabin which allowed for single occupancy

would also be installed, thereby allowing individuals the chance to sail on the ship without having to find a cabin mate or pay the additional supplement.

HAMBURG REFIT

Once plans for the *Oriana*'s refit were agreed, tenders were invited from the various shipyards that could do the work. P&O Cruises were keen to use a yard that had a proven track record in carrying out this type of conversion work and two European shipyards in particular were the front runners as both had carried out similar works to a great many cruise ships.

Of course the contract price was a main concern but the quality of the product and the time required to complete the job were other important factors in deciding who should carry out the refit. In the end it was announced that the German shipyard of Blohm and Voss in Hamburg had won the contract. The *Oriana* would go there for two weeks at the end of November 2011 and return to Southampton in time for a series of short cruises including her Christmas and New Year cruise around the Mediterranean before setting off on her annual Grand Voyage around the world.

Once the terms of the contract were agreed, preparation work began to make sure that everything was going to be in place so that when the ship arrived in Hamburg work could begin immediately on her conversion. Orders were placed with the various suppliers who would be providing the new materials for the conversion including Brintons of Kidderminster who had supplied all the original carpets on the *Oriana* when she was built back in 1995 and numerous subcontractors who would carry out some of the more specialist work such as the upgrading of the propulsion systems. What soon became apparent was that additional work was needed to be carried out on the ship in both the passenger and engineering spaces which simply could not be completed within the two-week period allotted for the ship to be out of service.

The main problem was that all the additional weight which was being added to the ship, mainly by the extra cabins on Deck 8, was going to affect the ship's stability and to correct this an extension to the hull in the form of what is known as a 'duck tail' was going to have to be fitted to the *Oriana*'s stern. However you looked at it, this was a lengthy procedure that could not be rushed so the decision was taken to cancel all of the pre-Christmas cruises and bring the ship back into service on 19th December 2011, almost three weeks after the original planned date. Of course the company were extremely disappointed at having to do this as they fully understood that no one likes to be told that their holiday has had to be cancelled but under the circumstances there simply was no other choice.

Top: In the early winter sunshine the **Oriana** *sits in the floating dock of the Blohm and Voss shipyard in Hamburg. (Blohm and Voss)*

Above: Taken from the River Elbe the **Oriana** *is seen towards the end of her conversion to an exclusively for adults ship in December 2011. (William Mayes)*

Right: Five years' worth of sea growth is removed from the **Oriana's** *hull by the means of high-pressure hoses. (Blohm and Voss)*

The *Oriana's* last cruise before her refit was a 16-night Eastern Mediterranean cruise which departed from Southampton on 31st October 2011. She arrived back on 16th November where a number of subcontractors boarded the ship in readiness for her departure to Hamburg.

Once she had left Southampton, work began to take out some of the furniture and carpets that were going to be replaced during the refit as well as removing the children's area ready to be converted into passenger accommodation. The *Oriana* arrived in Hamburg on the following evening's high tide at about 19.00 where upon all of her lifeboats were removed so that they could be

serviced and a new coat of gel applied to their hulls. As soon as they were removed, the yard's pilot boarded the ship and carefully manoeuvred her into dock number 11 which is the giant floating dock close to the city centre capable of holding ships of up to 250,000 tonnes. Once the *Oriana* was in position above her support blocks the ballast water in the floating dock was pumped out and as the floating dock slowly rose it gently made contact with the bottom of the *Oriana's* hull and the ship was carefully lifted out of the water. The ship continued to rise until the floor of the dry dock was out of the water and the *Oriana* sat about one metre above the level of the river. Once the ship was safely on her blocks various lines were put ashore

*Above left: The three bow thrusters at the front of the **Oriana** provide the ship with excellent manoeuvrability when used simultaneously with the other propulsion systems. (Brian D. Smith)*

*Above: A photograph from under the **Oriana**'s bow shows how perfectly symmetrical the ship's hull is at the water level. (Brian D. Smith)*

*Left: The new metal duck tail fitted to the **Oriana**'s hull was needed to compensate for the extra weight gained during the ship's conversion. (Brian D. Smith)*

including telephone and electrical supplies and an air bridge placed across her bow so that people could get access to her passenger accommodation.

NEW CABINS, RESTAURANTS AND A 'DUCK TAIL'

One of the first things on the agenda was to remove both of the *Oriana*'s variable pitch propellers and her stern propeller shafts, known as tail shafts. This was to allow the four blades of each propeller to be dismantled and opened up so that the internal workings could be cleaned and polished and for the stem seals around the propeller shafts, which stop sea water flooding into the ship, to be

replaced and upgraded. Work would also take place on the *Oriana*'s two rudders and stern thruster but this would take place with these in situ.

Whilst this carried on, work could now begin to mount the new £5 million, 360-tonne steel 'duck tail' that was to be fitted to the stern of the ship just above the waterline. A similar arrangement had taken place on the *Azura* during her construction as the amount of weight on her hull had increased over her sisters, including the *Ventura*, making the *Azura* the only one of the ten 'Grand Class' cruise ships to have a 'duck tail' fitted to her hull. This new feature did not improve fuel consumption or make the ship go any faster; it was there simply to improve stability. The 'duck tail' had

*Top: The **Queen Mary 2** was also in Germany whilst the **Oriana** was being refitted. The size difference between the two ships is very apparent in this photograph. (Blohm and Voss)*

Above: Part of the Conservatory self-service restaurant on Deck 11 was transformed into the Sorrento's Italian alternative dining venue with new tables and carpets. (Brian D. Smith)

Right: The former children's area was transformed into a new cabin area with 27 new cabins including single cabins and cabins with a private balcony. (Brian D. Smith)

been constructed at the yard before the *Oriana* arrived and was waiting for her on the quayside. Once the hull had been rubbed down and all the paint removed, large metal support brackets were attached to the hull and the new piece of the ship's hull lifted into position by one of the yard's giant cranes before being welded into place.

Inside the ship, crew members and contractors continued removing many of the ship's old carpets which were to be replaced as well as all the fixtures and fittings in the Spa on the Lido Deck and the children's play area on Deck 8. On the bridge and in the engine room the old propulsion system was stripped out and scaffolding was

erected around the external bridge wings as a new weather cover was to be installed over the top of the wings which would not completely enclose the wings, as with the other P&O Cruises ships, but would give the bridge officers some protection from the elements when docking the *Oriana*.

Work also got under way to transform the Curzon Room into a new select dining experience where a completely new gastronomic experience, designed by the celebrity chef Marco Pierre White would be introduced. Research carried out by P&O Cruises had shown that passengers wanted an entirely different select dining

Above left: The new Sorrento Restaurant with her tables set for her first dinner service on 19th December 2011. (Brian D. Smith)

*Above right: Another new feature for the **Oriana** was the Al Fresco Pizzeria situated next to the Riviera Pool where pizzas are freshly made on site. (Brian D. Smith)*

Left: A vibrant new carpet made by Brintons of Kidderminster was laid in the reception area which brightened up this important area immensely. (Brian D. Smith)

experience to that offered elsewhere on the ship and they also wanted it in a contemporary style similar to some of London's most famous restaurants such as Little Italy in Soho or Le Gavroche at Marble Arch, arguably London's finest Italian and French restaurants respectfully. Marco Pierre White had proved to be a huge success with passengers after he had worked his culinary magic on board some of the other P&O Cruises ships including the *Aurora* so it was decided to ask Marco to do it one more time on the *Oriana*. Named the Ocean Grill, the new restaurant would be given a new carpet of brown and caramel but the original light fittings and works of art including the elephant

statues and the Indian embroideries by Alice Kettle would remain. New plates, cutlery and glassware with the Ocean Grill emblem would also be added.

Another select dining venue was to be built on the port side of the ship's buffet restaurant called Sorrento's. Serving fine Italian food and wine this new establishment would also offer outside tables by the Terrace Bar giving passengers the option of eating al fresco when the weather permitted. Here new tables and chairs of wood and dusky red fabric would be installed as well as a new beige carpet which had a matching tree pattern of brown and red to help create a new vivid area which would be

*As dawn starts to break over the **Oriana**, shipyard lights allow work to continue on her conversion 24 hours a day. (YPS Peter Neumann/BVR)*

both warm and modern.

In the reception area, the black marble on the rear fascia of the reception desk was removed and was to be replaced with a light cream coloured marble which would brighten up this important area immensely. The dreary green carpet was to be replaced with a biscuit, brown and green-coloured patterned version in large swirls which transformed the ambience of what was a very dark and unimpressive area to one which would be bright, vibrant and thoroughly contemporary.

A NEW SPA

The Spa area was one of the areas on the ship that was to have the biggest transformation as all the art deco furniture in the relaxation area, including the cold stainless steel was removed as well as the circular fountain with the figure of a woman. In its place would be some high-quality relaxation furniture as the area was transformed into a new seating area for people waiting to use the private treatment rooms and was tastefully furnished in green and black which gave the area more of a natural look. The gymnasium was to receive a new wooden floor with full-length wall mirrors and the out-of-date mirrored ceiling replaced. The latest in cardiovascular equipment including cross trainers, running machines and cycling machines were

to be installed as well as new floor mats and computerised rowing machines. The health and beauty section was to have new hairdressing stations installed as well as a new foot spa and a complete revamp of the private treatment rooms with new fixtures and furniture which were to match the new furniture in the relaxation area.

Down on Deck 8, the large floor to ceiling windows in the former children's area were cut out and all traces of the Peter Pan play area and the Decibels teenage club were removed. In their place new services were installed which would provide electricity, water and air conditioning to the 27 new passenger cabins that were to be constructed in this area, including the 12 new cabins with their own private balcony taking the total number of balconied cabins on the Oriana to 130. Each cabin would be fitted out in a similar style to that of the rest of the ship with reminiscent wooden arches, flat screen TVs, plenty of wardrobe spaces and their own private bathrooms.

The Pacific Lounge was to get a complete makeover with new cream-coloured covers for the fixed seating and a dazzling red and cream swirled carpet surrounding the wooden dance floor. The dark wooden wall features were to be replaced with a softer material and a new mural of leaf stencils which would match the new red-coloured easy chairs to be arranged around the lower floor. A new lighting

system was to be installed above the stage and dance floor along with an enhanced sound system which would improve the acoustics and make the performances taking place in this room even more impressive than they already were.

Down in the engine room work had begun to replace a total of 45 tonnes of steel from the top of the steel blocks which go to make up the double bottom of the ship's hull known as the tank top. This is the lowest level of the ship to which anyone has access as the spaces below this are known as voids. All the heavy machinery which powers the ship such as the engines, gearboxes and generators sit on top of the tank top and over the years the vibration that is created in this large space tends to weaken the metal used in its construction. This is not an unusual occurrence and any large ship of a similar age to the *Oriana* will have to have this work carried out.

Additional work was to be carried out on the engines and other equipment which cannot normally be done whilst the ship is at sea. For example, the turbo charger on each of the engines is a huge piece of equipment that is attached to the exhaust system and cannot be removed whilst the ship is in service due to its size and position. Now was the perfect time to take each one out and to recondition it ready for another five years' service which is when the *Oriana* is next due to be dry-docked. Other work included replacing some of the cladding on the funnel uptakes and a complete service of the ships air conditioning and bilge systems. The new propulsion system meant a new computer system being added to the engine control room which would provide a more delicate operation of the ship's rudders and propellers with a more advanced monitoring system. On the bridge a new control panel was added to the main navigational console which was linked to this new system and gave the navigational officers the same information as was being received by the engineers in the engine control room.

Outside, the *Oriana*'s hull was given a full renovation with special attention being given to the area of the ship which is normally under water. Five years of algae and other sea growth, which affects a ship's performance, had attached itself to the metalwork and had to be blasted off with high-power water hoses. Once the hull had been cleaned a special paint called Intersleek was applied across the hull including the bulbous bow, rudders and stabilisers which not only protects the ship from the corrosive power of the sea but also forms a protective barrier against future sea growth and makes the ship's hull more slippery through the water thereby improving fuel economy. In total around 4,000 litres of paint were used to repaint the *Oriana* and to make sure she looked as new and beautiful as the day she entered service.

RETURN TO SERVICE

Eventually all the work that needed to be carried out

during the refit was completed and the ship was ready to go back into the sea. The tail shafts were reattached to the main propeller shafts and the propellers reassembled and attached to the ship. All the new engineering equipment was tested and commissioned before the final phase of their acceptance which could only take place once the ship had been through its sea trials which would start once she left the yard and was in the North Sea. All the new carpets were finally laid and all the new furniture for the two new restaurants was installed. The gymnasium equipment was put through its paces and the cabins were fitted out with all their soft furnishings such as the linen and curtains. Once all this was complete, the floating dock was flooded with seawater and the giant structure slowly settled back onto the seabed allowing the *Oriana* to float away once more. Her new 'duck tail' hardly made a difference to her overall appearance as did the new cabins on Deck 8 which were discretely blended in to the after end of the ship so that no one would notice any change here at all.

On 17th December 2011 the *Oriana* left Hamburg and headed back down the River Elbe to the North Sea at Cuxhaven where once clear of the European mainland she was subjected to a set of sea trials designed to put her new propulsion system through its paces and to see how the new 'duck tail' affected the ship's overall performance.

Everything went to plan and the *Oriana* started her journey back to Southampton, arriving off the Nab Tower in the Solent just after midnight on 19th December. She made her way up to the Mayflower Terminal in the early hours of the morning and began loading passengers for her Christmas and New Year cruise later that day. Once she had docked at her home port, several managers from P&O Cruises and invited members of the cruise and travel trade made their way on board and began a tour of the new ship. Everyone thought she looked fantastic and that the refit had gone a long way to improving and modernising the ambience on board. It was felt that the changes would continue to make the *Oriana* a very desirable ship for passengers to enjoy cruising on for the foreseeable future.

The *Oriana* has now been in service for over 17 years and is a very popular ship with both her passengers and crew. She has a loyal band of followers who no doubt will be very pleased with the ship's new look and the company's decision to spend so much money on her to bring her up to the standards required of a modern-day cruise ship. With her future assured, it is very good to know that the *Oriana* will be around for some time yet and we can all appreciate why so many people think she is one of the best cruise ships ever to be designed and built exclusively for the British market.

*The **Oriana** glides majestically past the Büyük Mecidiye Camii (Grand Imperial Mosque) of Sultan Abdülmecid which sits close to the Bosphorus Bridge in Istanbul which links Europe with Asia. (P&O Cruises)*

Reflections

BILL AND BRENDA MAYES FROM LONDON

Bill Mayes has been cruising with P&O Cruises since 1971 when he travelled with his parents on a seven-night cruise to Palma and Lisbon on board the original *Oriana*. It was in the era when passenger liners still travelled at good speeds even when cruising and the average speed for the run from Palma to Lisbon was around 26 knots. He immediately fell in love with this sort of holiday and, at the time of writing, has completed 73 cruises and spent over 1,000 nights at sea. It is fair to say that Bill has become something of an expert in cruise ships and he is now the Chairman of the Ocean Liner Society as well as the author of the popular annual 'Cruise Ships' which is published by Overview Press every summer.

Bill completed a further six cruises with P&O Cruises in the 1970s sailing on the original *Oriana*, the *Orsova* and the much loved *Canberra*. His future wife Brenda joined him for his 1977 cruise on the *Oriana* but to his disappointment, she failed to enjoy it as much as he did. This did not put him off as they were married a year later and happily celebrated their Pearl wedding anniversary in 2008.

Although his interest in cruising certainly did not diminish, the number of cruises in which he participated certainly did so. He subsequently opted for a few shorter cruises, either on his own or with his son Richard, but he did enjoy a family holiday on a Swan Hellenic cruise on the *Orpheus* in 1981. Luckily for Bill, things changed in 1994 when the new P&O Cruises brochure arrived advertising sailings on the new *Oriana*. "Brenda and I decided that we would give the new ship a try as I had been following the building of the ship with great interest," he told me. "Every few months a rather smart update booklet would arrive from P&O Cruises detailing what we could expect on the new ship. Richard and I went to Southampton to see the *Oriana* sail on her maiden voyage and were lucky enough to get onto the quayside as she departed, something that would be impossible to do today due to the increased security around the terminals. However, it was only a few short weeks before our first real cruise on the *Oriana* and a trip up to the Baltic. Arriving in Southampton and seeing the magnificent new ship towering over the passenger terminal caused great excitement amongst the three of us and before we knew it we were aboard and enjoying ourselves.

As we walked onto the ship I thought everything seemed perfect. It was a P&O Cruises ship, it smelt like a P&O Cruises ship and it felt like a P&O Cruises ship. Even the stewards were the traditional P&O Cruises Indian stewards with white gloves who took our luggage and showed us to our cabin and after a gap of 18 years without travelling on a P&O ship, I felt like I was home again. We loved the new ship and had a wonderful holiday. I couldn't wait to book another cruise on her so in 1998 we took our second cruise, this time to the Norwegian fjords. We again had a great time and were going to book another cruise on

Bill and Brenda Mayes. (William Mayes collection)

her but in the end decided to try the new *Aurora* to see if she was as wonderful as the *Oriana*."

In Bill's opinion, the *Aurora* is a well-built ship, and certainly is attractively fitted out, but for him the *Oriana* had the edge with her wonderful Curzon Room (the perfect place to sleep through a classical recital after dinner he says) and her forward unobstructed viewing deck. He considers the Anderson's Bar on the *Oriana* a better room than the similarly named bar on the *Aurora* and although the layout of the two ships is broadly similar he simply prefers the *Oriana* as she is just a magnificent ship in every way.

Bill and Brenda went back on the *Oriana* in 2001 (Black Sea), 2002 (Adriatic), 2004 (Eastern Mediterranean) and 2006 (Caribbean – round trip from Southampton) which made the *Oriana* not only their favourite cruise ship but the ship Bill has cruised on more than any other.

Now that she has been refitted he thinks it is time to go back again and see how she looks after her half-life conversion to an exclusively for adults ship.

JOHANNES AND MARGARET VAN BARREN FROM BATH

Johannes and Margaret Van Barren are big fans of P&O Cruises and over the years have been on more holidays with the company than they care to remember. What they know is that the service you receive on a P&O Cruises ship is second to none and the crews are always so friendly.

"Nothing seems too much trouble for them," says Margaret. "Whatever it is that we ask them they always do it so well and with a smile, it really does make a difference.

We have tried other cruise lines but they aren't the same, we will always use P&O Cruises and always the *Aurora*."

"We loved the old *Victoria* when she was with P&O," says Johannes, "but for us the *Aurora* is just about the best ship afloat; she is our second home. We love the decor of the ship, it is just so beautiful. I love sitting around the atrium having a drink and watching the world go by whilst reading a good book. It's simply wonderful."

Margaret continues, "We very much enjoy spending time in the Carmen's Lounge, especially the dancing. The dance floor is a good size and the dance instructors are extremely professional when we attend the many dance classes there. I also love the fact you can sit in the library which has some very comfortable chairs whilst you look out of those huge windows that go right up to the ceiling. It really is a great place to spend a sea day when the weather is not very good."

I ask them if they have been on the *Oriana*. "Oh yes," says Johannes, "but only the once. Of course she was a lovely ship but she wasn't the *Aurora*. We've been on the *Aurora* six times now and we have just booked ourselves on next year's 22-night cruise to the Caribbean on her. We would never use another ship, it would be like disserting an old friend," he laughs. "There is something about the *Aurora* which makes her so great but I can't quite put my finger on it. All I know is we love her and as long as she is in service we will continue to use her." His wife nods along in agreement and I for one know exactly what they mean.

NOEL CRAGGS AND LYNNE STARK FROM GUILDFORD, SURREY

Noel and Lynne have been keen cruisers most of their lives and make it a point to go cruising with P&O Cruises every year. They have sailed on the *Oriana* on nine previous occasions and plan to celebrate their tenth trip on the ship by sailing across the Atlantic on her to New York and New England next autumn. Their first ever cruise on a P&O ship was on the *Oriana* back in 1996 and since then they have tried most of the ships in the current P&O Cruises fleet but the *Oriana* is a personal favourite of theirs and is always the ship they choose when booking their annual holiday. One of Noel's biggest regrets in life was that he did not get the chance to sail on the *Canberra*.

"I don't know why we never did it," he says, "but for some reason we never booked a cruise on her. Every year we looked at going on her but we always ended up on a land holiday or choosing another ship. I really wish we had gone on her now but it's too late."

I ask them why the *Oriana* is their favourite ship and their replies are typical of the many passengers I have spoken to. "When you see the *Oriana* and you look at her beautiful outline you know you are going on a proper ship," says Noel.

Noel Craggs, Lynne Stark and their good friend Mohammed Sawab. (Brian D. Smith)

I ask Lynne if she agrees. She says, "To be totally honest I am not that bothered by what a ship looks like but where the *Oriana* is head and shoulders above every other ship we have ever sailed on is her beautiful atrium. It is so stunning. I also love the dinner service on board and the food is always delicious. We seem to enjoy every meal and always have breakfast and lunch in the waiter service restaurants rather than in the self-service restaurant. Quite why anyone would want to go self-service when you can be waited on hand and foot by those wonderful waiters is beyond me. There is nothing like it anywhere in the world. I get really sad on the day we get off and although you know you have had a great holiday I always get miserable when it's time to go home."

"We have used other cruise lines," continues Noel, "but they are simply not the same. I think we are P&O Cruises people and we just love our time on board, especially on the *Oriana*. She is over 15 years old now but she still looks magnificent and I know the crew work very hard looking after her. I hope she stays with the company for a very long time because it will be a very sad day when she's not in service. The atmosphere on board is unique. You feel like the crew are your personal friends as they always go that little bit further to make your time on board special. They are very friendly but not too informal. I have had some wonderful cruises on the *Oriana* over the years and some of my best memories are from being on board."

Lynne laughs and says, "We plan to be sailing on her for many years to come. I hope to retire in a few years and then we will be looking to do a world cruise on the *Oriana* or perhaps cruise down to Australia for a holiday in Sydney and Perth. It has always been a dream of mine to travel the world so I hope they won't get rid of her too soon."

Phillip and Jackie Chalke with their two children Samantha and Amy. (Brian D. Smith)

PHILLIP AND JACKIE CHALKE AND FAMILY FROM MANCHESTER

Philip Chalke and his family have completed eight holidays with P&O Cruises and sailed on three of their ships, the *Oceana*, the *Ventura* and the *Aurora*. Of these, six have been on the *Aurora*, which has become their favourite ship, and the one they like to call home. Once they tried sailing with an American cruise line but found that the ship and the food on board was not to their taste and as a result have promised only to use P&O Cruises in the future.

Philip explained, "The *Aurora* is such a beautiful ship that we just love being on board. I know that the kids will have a great time and leave Jackie and me alone to relax and get away from it all. The kids' clubs on board keep the children busy almost all of the day which means we can just relax by the pool and do nothing which the kids would find very boring. Personally my favourite part of the ship is the Crow's Nest Bar high up at the front of the ship, especially when the sea has some good waves on it and you can watch the bow of the ship ploughing through them. I find this very relaxing. At night my favourite place is Anderson's Bar but we only go in there on formal nights as it doesn't seem right to go in there unless you are dressed for the occasion. It's a rather special place for me. I call it the First Class bar due to its grand surroundings and the smartly dressed waiters. I always expect to see James Bond in there but I never have."

Jackie says, "The *Aurora* is just the perfect ship for a family like ours to go on for a holiday. Firstly we always get two cabins with interconnecting doors and that is important to me as I can keep a watchful eye on the kids. I never worry about them whilst we are on board as the youth crew take care of everything. The girls are always telling me about their days and what they get up to whether its competitions in the swimming pool or having a party in the restaurant. It's also nice to know that if the kids don't fancy getting dressed up for dinner then we can drop them off at the youth club and the staff will look after them until Phil and I have finished our romantic dinner alone."

"You have to admit," says Phillip, "the *Aurora* is pretty romantic, I mean having a drink out on the open deck before dinner which is very enjoyable but the feeling you get as you walk down the staircase into dinner as the waiters guide you to your table, well it makes you feel like Royalty. You only get that on the *Aurora*, I don't know if it's a subconscious thing or what but no ship makes me feel as happy and relaxed when I am on holiday as being on the *Aurora* does."

I ask Jackie what makes the vessel so special for her. She replies, "It's just the beautiful decor all around the ship. Everything is so lovely and welcoming no matter where you go. The restaurants are a good example. On our last cruise we were in the Medina Restaurant and I know Phillip has mentioned the lovely staircase you use to enter the restaurant but everything else about it is lovely too. The furniture, the waiters, the food, in fact everything in there is just brilliant."

I ask Sam what is it like for a teenager being on board. She says, "It's fantastic. I can choose to do my own thing or go down to the club. Some days I just like to sunbathe and go swimming but on other days I like the themed activities that take place. We had a night in the nightclub (Masquerades) on our last cruise and that was really good as the DJ plays all the latest records including Rihanna and Beyonce. I was really surprised but absolutely loved it. I tell my friends at school all about the *Aurora* and I wish I could take them with me."

The youngest of the family, Amy is a bit of a sports enthusiast and she explains why she loves the ship so much. "They have great sports on the ship with tennis and water basketball in our own swimming pool where no adults are allowed. We've played five-a-side football too and that was great fun as is everything we do on the ship. I don't know much about the facilities on the other ships but on the *Aurora* we always seem to have lots of fun."

Phillip says, "We still like to go on holiday as a family and on the *Aurora* we are all very happy. We have enjoyed many great times on board and I know that when we go to book our next holiday we will look at the *Aurora* before anything else, it's just something we always do.

JOHN AND HAZEL AMOS FROM WEST WYCOMBE, KENT

John Amos is a recently retired police officer who has had a wonderful career with the Metropolitan Police Force. Since his retirement he has become something of a cruise ship enthusiast and spends his spare time equally split between this and his other great passion, the Great War. John and Hazel have been on seven cruises on the *Aurora* and have also sailed on the *Azura* and the *Arcadia*. They have never considered sailing with another cruise line as they are so happy with the service they receive from the crews on a P&O Cruises ship that they just could not imagine sailing with anyone else.

"We have special affection for *Aurora* as she was the first cruise ship that we ever sailed on," John explains. "We had been told that she is a happy ship and we were not disappointed. You normally find that the majority of passengers sailing on her have done so before because *Aurora* is their favourite ship and because they enjoy the friendly atmosphere on board."

It is true that a lot of people enjoy sailing on the *Aurora* so much that they do tend to book another cruise on her rather than another ship. The number of passengers returning to sail on the *Aurora* is higher than any other ship in the P&O Cruises fleet.

Hazel says, "The *Aurora* is big enough to be special but not too big to be impersonal. She has the atmosphere of

John and Hazel Amos. (Brian D Smith)

the liners from the glory days of cruising whilst having every modern convenience. For me, one of the factors that goes towards this special atmosphere is the Promenade Deck. Unlike a lot of other cruise ships you can do a complete circumnavigation of the ship on this one deck and as you go round you not only see other regular exercisers but also those taking in the sun on the loungers and deckchairs. Often you might only exchange a casual wave or a nod but it all adds to the feeling of belonging on the ship. The Promenade Deck is great for burning off both the extra pounds that you put on at dinner the night before and the guilty feelings that you suffer for having over indulged – 3.2 circuits is the equivalent of a mile so it is very easy to calculate how far you have travelled."

I ask John if this is one of the reasons he likes the ship so much. "It's not just this but also the fact that the *Aurora* has so much open deck space at her stern which makes her special," he replies. "The best place to have a Sail Away Party is at the rear of the ship so that you can watch the port slowly recede into the distance as you head out to sea again. We have very fond memories of sailing out of New York as the sun set behind all those famous skyscrapers. We have also found the *Aurora*'s crew to be very friendly people and this goes a long way to making our cruises extra special."

John tells me about an occasion where a member of the restaurant crew went just that little bit further to make their cruise a very memorable occasion. "On one cruise we complimented our table waiter on his napkin creations and asked him to show us how to fold that evening's offering. He obliged with great patience and humour. Every subsequent evening he took the time to teach us one or

Lynn Hammond. (Brian D Smith)

two more. He took great pleasure in doing this despite the fact that we were second sitting and that by doing so he delayed clearing our table and setting up for breakfast."

Hazel sums up their feelings for the ship by simply saying, "When we are deciding on which cruise to go on we always look first to see where *Aurora* is going before looking at anything else. She is our ship of choice above any other."

LYNN HAMMOND FROM FARNBOROUGH, HAMPSHIRE

Being a single person it is particularly important to Lynn to go on the right sort of holiday where there are lots of opportunities to get to meet new people and interact with other like-minded individuals. She has been cruising with P&O Cruises for 17 years and in that time the *Oriana* has become her favourite ship to travel on.

"What particularly appeals to me on the *Oriana* is the way she seems to attract the sort of people I like mixing with and her wonderful public rooms where we can enjoy ourselves," she explains. "Especially the gymnasium and spa area which are situated right below the Crow's Next Bar. This way I can enjoy a morning in the spa followed by an afternoon socialising and enjoying a drink upstairs and all with the most superb views over the front of the ship. I like to stay fit and pamper myself and having good surroundings is just as important as having a good masseuse or the right equipment to work out on and the *Oriana* seems to have the perfect balance. I find most of her public rooms very intimate and interesting, especially all the old paintings of the P&O ships from the 19th century. The Lord's Tavern is another great place to socialise and have a drink because of

its outside terrace which apart from the wonderful views out to sea provides some welcome shade when it's hot and much needed shelter when its raining."

Lynn's advice to anyone travelling alone is to ask for a large table at dinner as this is the best way of meeting other people. "Over the years I have met up with many wonderful people who have become firm friends, so much so that one or two of us now go cruising together. The crew do a wonderful job of introducing you to other people and if by some chance you don't get on with the people at your table they go to great lengths to move you to a more suitable table."

Lynn tells me that she thinks that all of the crew are absolutely fabulous, especially the cabin stewards whom she wishes she could take home with her as they put her housekeeping to shame. "When I am travelling as a lone female they all seem to take that little bit of extra care to look after me. They organise so many events on sea days such as dance classes in the Pacific Lounge, playing card lessons in Crichton's (I have become quite a good poker player thanks to my lessons on the ship) and even swimming lessons in the pool. With all these activities going on you cannot help but meet new people and start a new friendship or perhaps something else.

"I have even enjoyed a little romance on the *Oriana* after I met a particularly nice gentleman who was also travelling alone. It turned out that he went to school just down the road from me and we had been near neighbours for over 20 years and never knew each other. We had an exceptionally good cruise together and I can honestly say that some of the 16 nights we were together on the ship were some of the most wondrous of my life. Cruising on the *Oriana* can do this for you and I cannot imagine a land-based holiday where you would get the opportunity to meet so many people on one holiday. We are still in touch and there is a distinct possibility of us going on another cruise together later this year.

"When you see the *Oriana* next to most cruise ships she does look so much more graceful than they do with a timeless classic appearance of what I think a ship should look like. I am always telling my friends that you can't have a bad holiday on such a great ship and to this day I have never been proved wrong.

"I have seen people getting married whilst on board and it all looks so romantic. I do dream that one day I will get married at sea. If I do, it will be on the *Oriana* as it's such a great ship and definitely my favourite ship to go cruising on."

*A truly spectacular sight as the **Aurora** passes under the Golden Gate Bridge and out into the Pacific Ocean. (P&O Cruises)*

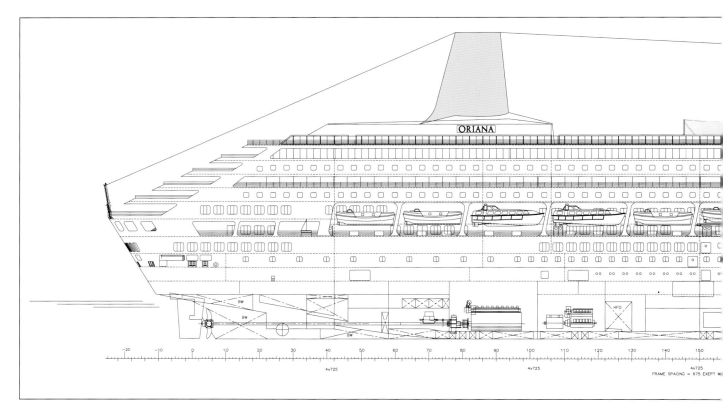

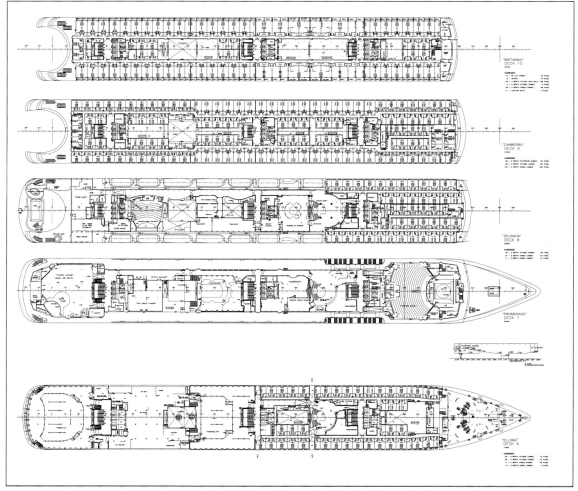

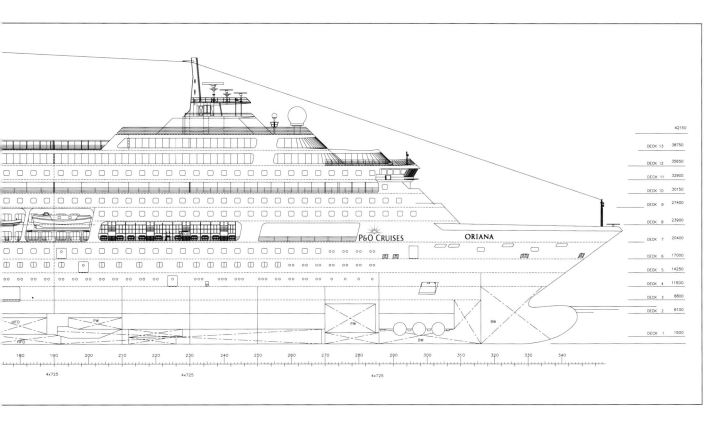

Deck markings (right side): 42150, DECK 13 38750, DECK 12 35650, DECK 11 32900, DECK 10 30150, DECK 9 27400, DECK 8 23900, DECK 7 20400, DECK 6 17000, DECK 5 14250, DECK 4 11500, DECK 3 8800, DECK 2 6100, DECK 1 1500

Labels: P&O CRUISES, ORIANA

General Information

Builders: Meyer Werft of Papenburg, Germany.

Yard Number: 636

Contract Signed: December 1991

Contract Price: £200 Million

Lead Design Architect: Robert Tillberg

Date of Keel Laying Ceremony: 11th March 1993

Date of Float Up: 27th July 1994

Date of Delivery: 2nd April 1995

Date of Naming Ceremony: 6th April 1995

Ship's Godmother: Her Majesty Queen Elizabeth II.

Date of Maiden Voyage: 9th April 1995

Call Sign: ZCDU9

IMO Number: 9050137

Classification: Lloyds Register +100A1 Passenger Ship.

Country of Registration: Bermuda

Passenger Capacity: 1812

Officers and Crew: 762

Technical Information

Gross Tonnage: 69,840 Tonnes

Net Tonnage: 37,559 Tonnes

Maximum Displacement Tonnage: 38018.9 Tonnes

Deadweight Tonnage: 5818.9 Tonnes

Length o.a: 260.00 Metres   Length p.p: 224.05 Metres

Breadth: 32.2 Metres

Design Draught: 7.9 Metres   Maximum Draught 8.30 Metres

Number of Decks: 14   Passenger Decks 10

Engines: 2 X MAN BW 9L 58/64; 2 X MAN BW 6L 58/64

Total Engine Output: 54,054 BHP

Diesel Generators: 4 X MAN BW 6L 40/54

Electrical Output: 26,080 KW

Propellers: 2 x 4 Variable pitch bladed LIPS 5.8 Metre diameter

Thrusters: LIPS 1,500KW 3 Bow 1 Stern

Maximum Speed: 26 Knots

Service Speed: 24 Knots

Average Fuel Consumption: 180 Tonnes of heavy fuel oil per day.

Cabins

8 Suites, 16 Mini Suites, 106 De-lux Cabins, 472 Outside Cabins with a window, 331 Inside Cabins, 8 Disabled Cabins

Main Public Rooms

Oriental Restaurant: 524 Seats

Peninsular Restaurant: 480 Seats

The Conservatory: 328 Seats

The Ocean Grill: 90 Seats

Sorrento's Restaurant: 94 Seats Inside, 60 Seats Outside

Theatre Royal : 680 Seats

Pacific Lounge: 450 Seats

Chaplin's Cinema: 189 Seats

Crows Nest: 300 Seats

The Lord's Tavern: 63 Seats

Anderson's Bar: 128 Seats

Harlequins Room: 220 Seats

Tiffany Court: 100 Seats

Thackeray Room: 12 Seats

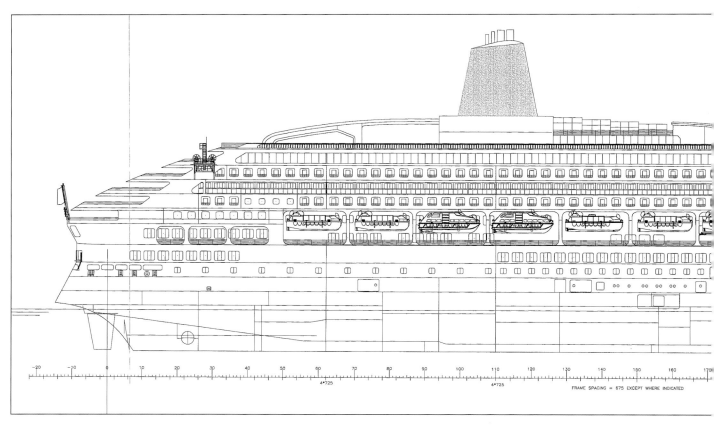

4*725   4*725   FRAME SPACING = 575 EXCEPT WHERE INDICATED

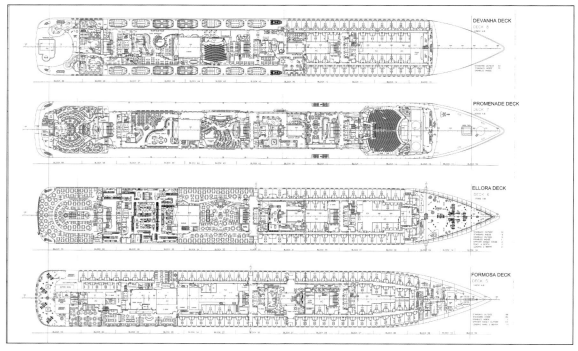

DEVANHA DECK
DECK 8

PROMENADE DECK
DECK 7

ELLORA DECK
DECK 6

FORMOSA DECK
DECK 5

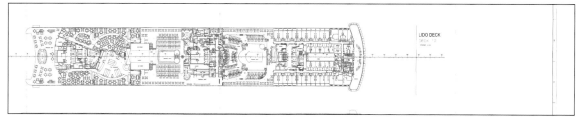

LIDO DECK
DECK 9

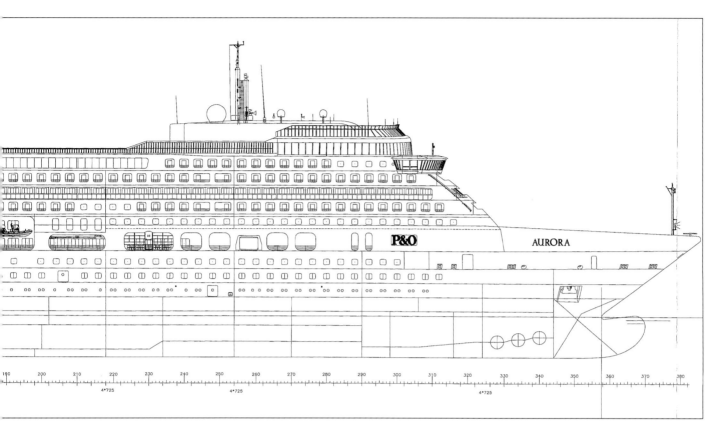

General Information

Builders: Meyer Werft of Papenburg, Germany.

Yard Number: 640

Contract Signed: April 1997

Contract Price: £200 Million

Lead Design Architect: Robert Tillberg

Date of Keel Laying Ceremony: 15th December 1998

Date of Float Out: 6th January 2000

Date of Delivery: 15th April 2000

Date of Naming Ceremony: 27th April 2000

Ship's Godmother: The Princess Royal, Princess Anne.

Date of Maiden Voyage: 1st May 2000

Call Sign: ZCDW9

IMO Number: 9169524

Classification: Lloyds Register +100A1 Passenger Ship.

Country of Registration: Bermuda

Passenger Capacity: 1878

Officers and Crew: 936

Technical Information

Gross Tonnage: 76,152 Tonnes

Net Tonnage: 40,037 Tonnes

Maximum Displacement Tonnage: 43,405 Tonnes

Deadweight Tonnage : 6,450 Tonnes

Length o.a:270.0 Metres   Length p.p: 242.6 Metres

Breadth: 32.2 Metres   Design Draught: 7.90 Metres

Maximum Draught 8.40 Metres

Number of Decks: 14   Number of Passenger Decks: 10

Engines: 4 X MAN BW 14V 48/60

Total Engine Output: 79,945 BHP

Electrical Output: 58,800 KW   Shaft Output: 40,000 KW

Propellers: 2 x 5 Fixed bladed KaMeWa 5.8 Metre diameter

Thrusters: LIPS 1,500KW 3 Bow 1 Stern

Maximum Speed: 29 Knots   Service Speed: 24 Knots

Fuel Consumption Average: 200 Tonnes of heavy fuel oil per day.

Cabins

2 Penthouse Suites, 10 Suites, 18 Mini Suites, 96 De-lux Cabins

272 Twin Cabins with a balcony, 239 Outside Cabins with a window

280 Inside Cabins, 22 Disabled Cabins

Main Public Rooms

Medina Restaurant: 528 Seats

Alexandra Restaurant: 520 Seats

The Orangery: 418 Seats

Cafe Bordeaux: 124 Seats

Curzon Theatre: 668 Seats

Carmens Lounge: 447 Seats

Playhouse Cinema: 210 Seats

Masquerades: 200

Crows Nest: 271 Seats

Champions Sports Bar: 125 Seats

Anderson's Bar: 126 Seats

Raffles Chocolate and Coffee Bar: 62 Seats

Charlies Champagne Bar: 19 Seats

Vanderbilt's: 104 Seats

*Sailing eastbound in the Panama Canal the **Oriana** is heading for the Atlantic Ocean and one of the greatest sea journeys of all time. (P&O Cruises)*

Acknowledgements

The author would like to thank P&O Cruises' Managing Director Carol Marlow for supporting this project and agreeing to write the Foreword, and also expresses his thanks to David Strawford, the Fleet Services Director for Carnival UK who has repeatedly given up his valuable time to help with many requests. He also acknowledges his sincere gratitude to Steve Morant of P&O Ferries who spent many hours talking him through the complexities of a modern-day cruise ship.

A mention must also be made to retired Royal Navy engineer Jim Hunter to whom the author is very grateful for providing so many of his original drawings and diagrams of both ships which now grace this book.

Thanks must also go to Captain Neil Turnbull of P&O Cruises who took time out of his busy schedule to accommodate many requests for photographs and information. Thanks are also due to Maurice Lowman, Nick Shooter and Richard Vie of Carnival UK along with James Cusick and Kate Rist of P&O Cruises for their assistance and help with numerous requests for all sorts of information associated with this project. The crews of both the *Oriana* and *Aurora* were so welcoming on every occasion that the author visited them. They are an extremely hard working group of talented people who are dedicated to providing their passengers with the best possible cruise experience.

From the Meyer Werft shipyard Mr Peter Hackmann and Mr Thomas Witolla for their time and allowing access to the yard's photo library and provided images of the ships under construction.

Finally, the author would like to thank John Hendy, for editing his completed manuscript, and Miles Cowsill of Ferry Publications who has done a magnificent job putting together yet another wonderful publication to add to his ever growing library of high-quality maritime books..